THERON Q.

(WILLIAM WALKER ATKINSON'S PSEUDONYM)

THE ART AND THE SCIENCE

OF

PERSONAL MAGNETISM

1913

"When man found himself fallen from this splendor, and was condemned to the unfortunate condition in which he is now reduced, his first rights were not abolished, they were only suspended, and he always retained the power to work and achieve by his efforts to restore them to their first value."

THE UNKNOWN PHILOSOPHER
IN "OF ERRORS AND TRUTH"
COLLECTION "ORIGINS OF MARTINISM"

WITH A PRACTICAL SUPPLEMENT IN MENTAL SCIENCES THAT BRINGS THREE EXERCISES FOR DEVELOPING YOUR PERSONAL MAGNETISM TO THE HIGHEST DEGREE AND PROVEN IN THEIR EFFECTS. SUPPLEMENT WRITTEN BY CHARLES LUCIEN DE LIÈVRE.

1st Edition in English in Brazil

THOT
Grupo Editorial

THE ART AND THE SCIENCE OF PERSONAL MAGNETISM

Author:
Theron Q, Dumont (pseudonym)
Author's real name:
William Walker Atkinson
Date of Birth:
December 5, 1862.
Date of Death:
November 22, 1932.
Title of this Work in English Original:
The Art and the Science of Personal Magnetism
Subtitle:
With a Practical Supplement in Mental Sciences written by Charles Lucien de Lièvre
Year and Place of the First English Edition:
1913, Paris, France
Editor of the Original Book in 1908:
Advanced Thought Publishing CO.
Digitization of the Original in English in Brazil:
Grupo Thot Editorial
Cover and Content Layout:
Grupo Thot Editorial
Review and General Supervision:
Charles Lucien de Lièvre
Chief Publisher in Brazil:
Carlos Sérgio Cavassana
Year, Place of the English Edition in Brazil:
2022, Taubaté, São Paulo, Brazil.
Translation into Portuguese, French, Italian and Spanish:
Charles Lucien de Lièvre
Birth date:
May, 8 1964.
Death date:
I still don't have one because I'm very much alive and intend to

continue writing and translating for Amazon for decades to come.

Collection and Number of this Volume:
Mental Sciences in Practice – Volume 3

PUBLIC DOMAIN DATA AND VERIFICATION LINKS
1. Link containing the biographical data of the author and his works:
https://en.wikipedia.org/wiki/William_Walker_Atkinson
2. Link that brings details of the author's life, his spiritual trajectory and his works:
https://theosophy.wiki/en/William_Walker_Atkinson
3. Link with some biographical data of the author's birth, death and life:
https://www.successconsciousness.com/blog/concentration-mind-power/william-walker-atkinson/
4. Link to William Walker Atkinson's biographical data, birth, death and his mystical career, as well as all the pseudonyms under which he wrote his vast work:
https://www.encyclopedia.com/people/philosophy-and-religion/other-religious-beliefs-biographies/william-walker-atkinson

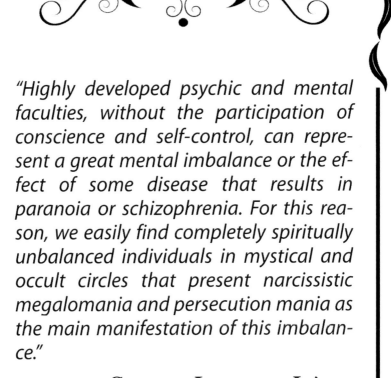

"Highly developed psychic and mental faculties, without the participation of conscience and self-control, can represent a great mental imbalance or the effect of some disease that results in paranoia or schizophrenia. For this reason, we easily find completely spiritually unbalanced individuals in mystical and occult circles that present narcissistic megalomania and persecution mania as the main manifestation of this imbalance."

**CHARLES LUCIEN DE LIÈVRE
EM "PSYCHIC DISORDERS"**

THERON Q. DUMONT

(WILLIAM WALKER ATKINSON'S PSEUDONYM)

THE ART AND THE SCIENCE
OF
PERSONAL MAGNETISM

1913

"When man found himself fallen from this splendor, and was condemned to the unfortunate condition in which he is now reduced, his first rights were not abolished, they were only suspended, and he always retained the power to work and achieve by his efforts to restore them to their first value."

THE UNKNOWN PHILOSOPHER
IN "OF ERRORS AND TRUTH"
COLLECTION "ORIGINS OF MARTINISM"

WITH A PRACTICAL SUPPLEMENT IN MENTAL SCIENCES THAT BRINGS THREE EXERCISES FOR DEVELOPING YOUR PERSONAL MAGNETISM TO THE HIGHEST DEGREE AND PROVEN IN THEIR EFFECTS. SUPPLEMENT WRITTEN BY CHARLES LUCIEN DE LIÈVRE.

1st Edition in English in Brazil

THOT
Grupo Editorial

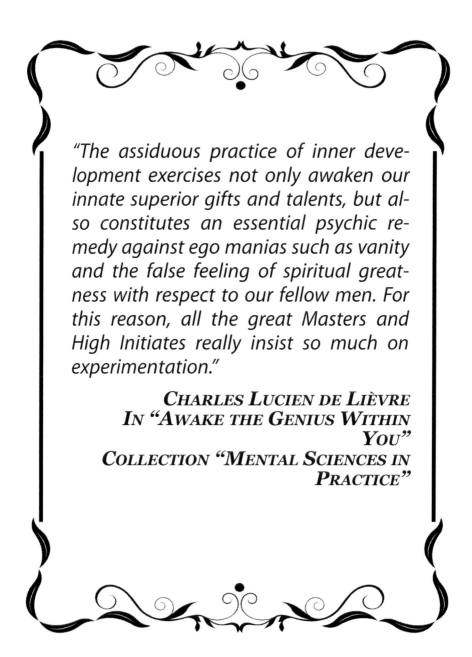

"The assiduous practice of inner development exercises not only awaken our innate superior gifts and talents, but also constitutes an essential psychic remedy against ego manias such as vanity and the false feeling of spiritual greatness with respect to our fellow men. For this reason, all the great Masters and High Initiates really insist so much on experimentation."

CHARLES LUCIEN DE LIÈVRE
IN "AWAKE THE GENIUS WITHIN YOU"
COLLECTION "MENTAL SCIENCES IN PRACTICE"

TABLE OF CONTENTS

Part 1 – Containing an introduction to this Collection as well as a set of advice and tips on how to conduct your mystical path into practice. The translator also presents a Practical Supplement that brings three exercises to improve your personal magnetism.

Part 2 – Containing the theory and practices as exposed by William Walker Atkinson.

PART 1

Containing an introduction to this Collection as well as a set of advice and tips on how to conduct your mystical path into practice. The translator also presents a Practical Supplement that brings three exercises to improve your personal magnetism.

"The Mental Sciences can only be verified on the basis of our individual experimentation. There are no other means, because our mental powers manifest from the inside out and respond directly to the mental stimuli we give them through systematic exercises and assiduous practice."

CHARLES LUCIEN DE LIÈVRE
IN "AWAKE THE GENIUS WITHIN YOU"
COLLECTION "MENTAL SCIENCES IN PRACTICE"

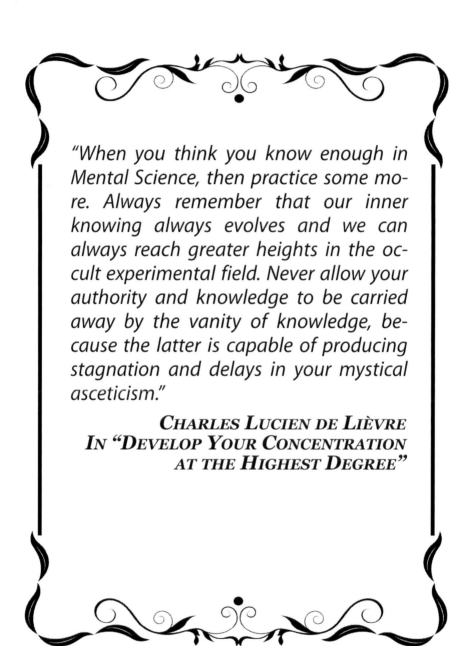

"When you think you know enough in Mental Science, then practice some more. Always remember that our inner knowing always evolves and we can always reach greater heights in the occult experimental field. Never allow your authority and knowledge to be carried away by the vanity of knowledge, because the latter is capable of producing stagnation and delays in your mystical asceticism."

CHARLES LUCIEN DE LIÈVRE
IN "DEVELOP YOUR CONCENTRATION AT THE HIGHEST DEGREE"

COLLECTION "MENTAL SCIENCES IN PRACTICE"

"As long as man lowers himself to the condition of a pure biological being, he will remain lost and will suffer constantly in this Region of the Sensitive, with the only certainty being the death of his physical being; nothing else. When he resolutely decides to work on himself to know his true nature, then he will transcend death and all the weaknesses that limit and enslave him to this material world, gathering in himself all the scattered parts of his immortal being to reassume the place that Creator had destined him from the Beginning of Things."

S:: I::

This third volume of our Collection presents even more practical aspects of an energy that we are all carriers of: personal magnetism. And like all our other gifts and talents, this one too is capable of development through regular exercise, self-discipline, perseverance, determination and, above all, a powerful SOVEREIGN WILL.

Of all the primitive rights that were suspended from us in this Sensitive Region, only one of them remained active and at the total disposal of man so that he could restore the others to their first value: the WILL. It is in this precious gift of the soul that all the strength of our

FREEDOM and the essential equality between us and our fellow beings with whom we share this material plane and this brief physical existence are found. Note carefully these words of the Unknown Philosopher who already in the 18th century pointed out this possibility to us:

> *"When man found himself fallen from this splendor, and was condemned to the unhappy condition in which he is now reduced, his first rights were not abolished, they were only suspended, and he always retained the power to work and achieve by his efforts to restore them to their first value."*
>
> THE UNKNOWN PHILOSOPHER
> IN *"OF ERRORS AND TRUTH"*
> COLLECTION *"MARTINISM WITHOUT MYSTERIES"*

There are no men without WILL, there are only those who do not recognize it or have forgotten that it exists, so they feel lost in this Region of the Sensitive. Therefore, the penalty imposed on man because of his fall was that of "earning his bread in the sweat of his own face." Note that in this punishment, if we do not interpret it to the rigor of the dead letter, it teaches us the infinite love of the Creator towards his creature by applying to him, through his Infinite Justice, the Law of Effort, since it is only through it that we stimulate this talent of our soul and that we can regain, through this awakening, all our first rights. For this reason, "earning bread by the sweat of one's brow" means much more than working for the sustenance of our physical being, it means working to "earn and eat the bread of the spirit" that is so accessible to us, but which we refuse to see because we are so attached to this material reality.

One of the objectives of this Collection is to remember this precious gift in man so that, through constant exercise, he may be able to stimulate it and place it again at his service, recovering through this enormous power that identifies him with the Creator and empowered with his first rights, so that he can return with full consciousness to his First State of Glory.

The works of William Walker Atkinson were specially chosen to compose this Collection due to the gigantic practical character they bring to the sincere seeker, because there is no point in having a gigantic erudition in everything that concerns the Mental Sciences, when one remains idly by doing nothing to prove such theories. You only risk becoming an arrogant, narcissistic fool with a mania for spiritual greatness, but who remains even more lost in this Region of the Sensitive than the most common among men. Don't be such a fool!

So, get to work, because much work still awaits you and time is precious, since we are all imprisoned in it in this Region of the Sensitive.

CHARLES LUCIEN DE LIÈVRE
CREATOR AND ORGANIZER OF THE COLLECTION "MENTAL SCIENCES IN PRACTICE"

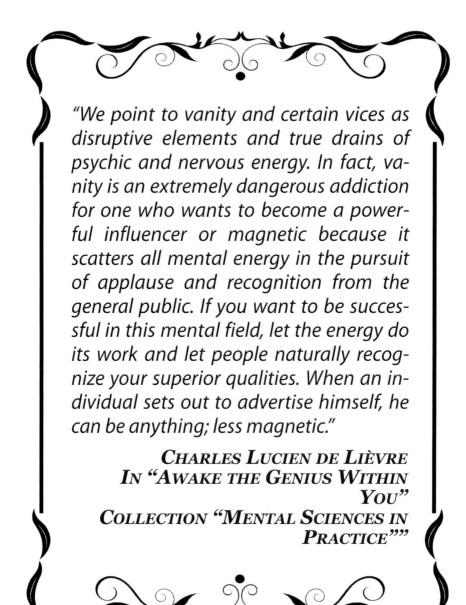

"We point to vanity and certain vices as disruptive elements and true drains of psychic and nervous energy. In fact, vanity is an extremely dangerous addiction for one who wants to become a powerful influencer or magnetic because it scatters all mental energy in the pursuit of applause and recognition from the general public. If you want to be successful in this mental field, let the energy do its work and let people naturally recognize your superior qualities. When an individual sets out to advertise himself, he can be anything; less magnetic."

CHARLES LUCIEN DE LIÈVRE
IN "AWAKE THE GENIUS WITHIN
YOU"
COLLECTION "MENTAL SCIENCES IN
PRACTICE"""

PREFACE TO THE ENGLISH EDITION

"Always keep in mind that with each step you take towards your self-realization, the whole of humanity takes this step with you, for just as all marine creatures are linked to each other by a common element that is water, man is connected to all other human beings and to their Creator by a common element far superior to what exists in this material world: an ocean of mind."

S:: I::

This is one of the most impressive works by William Walker Atkinson because, in addition to revealing to us a force of which we are already bearers, it shows us practical ways to stimulate it to a much higher degree of manifestation, so that we can put it at our service even in this material world, reconciling our higher and lower reality to generate success, peace and happiness for ourselves and everyone around us.

There is no doubt that man becomes much happier when he discovers and experiences the superior capacities of which he already possesses. This rediscovery brings much more happiness than the meeting of your first love, because even if it is intense, it is not lasting and is subject to the variations of time and space to which we are all subjected in this Sensitive Region.

Man, since his emergence on this Material Plane, yearns for something greater than this life in matter, dreams of this immortality to which he clings without knowing where this deep feeling comes from that torments him all the time and makes him seek in religions a relief for this pain that he experiences as a kind of nostalgia for a far superior condition he once enjoyed and to which he desperately longs to return. Louis-Claude de Saint-Martin, the Unknown Philosopher, tells us about this intuitive perception in man in one of his most important works:

> *"In this state of reprobation where man is condemned to crawl, and where he sees only the veil and the shadow of the true light, he retains more or less the memory of his glory, he nourishes more or less the desire to ascend there, all by reason of the free use of his intellectual faculties, by reason of the works which are prepared for him by justice, and of the employment which he must have in the work."*
>
> *THE UNKNOWN PHILOSOPHER*
> *IN "OF ERRORS AND TRUTH"*
> *COLLECTION "MARTINISM WITHOUT MYSTERIES"*

In the presentation of this Collection, we talked about the biblical adage "earning bread by the sweat of one's brow" and we went much further when referring to this bread, not just as material sustenance, but the "bread of the spirit" that can be won back by our personal efforts when we focus our eyes in the right direction: within us.

It is also for this reason that this entire Collection is based on theoretical knowledge and practical experimentation, as knowledge solidifies and evolves as our individual experiences become capable of proving theories. It is at this point that knowledge ceases to be "pure theory" or "speculation" to become "Wisdom".

∴

Bringing theory and practice together is not a very simple task, as the reader will perceive throughout this work and many others, because our mind, unprepared and totally accustomed to the lack of discipline, imposes limits and a strong resistance to practice, in addition to distrust with regarding the effectiveness of the proposed exercises.

> *"We always have to fight the worst demons that work against our evolution: those that we ourselves create when we give in to addictions and temptations. Among the most powerful are physical and mental laziness, followed by negligence and vanity. However, they can all be subjected to a power that none of them can resist: our WILL."*
>
> *S:: I::*

We have to impose a gigantic challenge and openly fight against these resistances, since they are the children of our own vices and idiosyncrasies.

The feeling of defeat that we experience throughout the practice stems precisely from two great vices: mental and physical laziness. Added to these are self-indulgence, neglect, and lack of confidence in our own superior innate capacities.

We have to be strong and face them all. The first step towards this achievement is recognizing that they are our creations and exist only in our minds. The second step is to take action and practice the exercises with perseverance and determination, even if disbelief ruminates in our minds. As the highly positive results present themselves, our consciousness gives way to an inner conviction that grows out of observing these results. In the first moment, it is necessary to trust absolutely in the author's guidelines, resist the temptations of giving up and complacency in order to, only later, obtain positive results.

"Always remember that the WILL is to the Sage what FAITH is to the common man. In reality, the WILL is nothing more than CONSCIOUS FAITH."

S:: I::

Anyone who has ever practiced concentration exercises will immediately recognize what has been said above about the temptations and resistances imposed by a mind accustomed to indiscipline. Therefore, if you want to feel the strength of your inner enemies in the flesh, we recommend that you start all your work by developing a powerful mental concentration (see also "Develop Your Concentration to the Highest Degree" by Charles Lucien de Lièvre)

It is by the mastery of inner temptations and vices that any external influence is also mastered. And this the reader will see throughout this work, in addition to the many others that make up this Collection. External forces depend on our greater or lesser power to resist or stop them. Every time we feel weak, we open the door for such external forces to have dominion over us. When we exercise our latent superior abilities, we build an enormous wall capable of protecting us from the attacks of our enemies. However, it is of fundamental importance that man recognizes the power he has over all of them from his conscience and from the use he can make of his innate superior capacities, knowing in advance that they do not awaken on their own.

Mental Sciences are all about this inner awakening, and we have to stick to it if we want to recover what we really are even in this Region of the Sensitive.

CHARLES LUCIEN DE LIÈVRE

INTRODUCTION

"Masters, mystery schools and books are only facilitators of the arduous task that we have in front of us in order to promote ourselves inwardly and recover our first rights; they're not its executors. This competence is our sole responsibility, therefore, it is non-transferable. This is what those who seek in Mental Sciences for proof of their veracity must stick to."

S:: I::

O ne thing is more than certain in the Mental Sciences, when we embrace methodical and systematic experimentation we get able to achieve great and positive results. However, these results can only be achieved by each of us individually. In other words, it is not possible to transmit evolution, inner growth and progress to another person, each of us must conquer his own through his personal efforts. We have to look to examples that inspire us and guide our steps, but the work of carrying out our mystical asceticism is always ours.

If this premise is understood right from the start, we will have taken an important step towards our self-realization and towards the correct use of our WILL which is, according to most of the Great Masters and Great Adepts of the past, the driving force of all our evolution and interior progress. For this reason, both

mental laziness and negligence become powerful enemies of our progress in any way. It is from this neglect
that evil takes its origin, because outside our vices and
limitations, such evils have no tangible existence. Meditate on these words of Saint-Martin that point us to
the true origin of evil:

> *"If it is by letting his will degenerate that the intelli-
> gent and free Being (man) acquires the knowledge
> and the feeling of evil, we must assure that evil has
> no other principle, nor any other origin than the very
> will of this free Being."*
>
> THE UNKNOWN PHILOSOPHER
> IN "OF ERRORS AND TRUTH"
> COLLECTION "MARTINISM WITHOUT MYSTERIES"

And we cannot forget the great lesson about Mental
Laws that the vampire legend brings us regarding our
individual responsibility for everything that concerns
our inner advancement and the likely action of evil on
us: "a vampire can only enter our house (heart and
mind) when he is invited by ourselves." Interpreting
this myth in a broader and more esoteric way, we can
say that evil invades us only when it finds the opening
that we give it on our own.

William Walker Atkinson develops these same concepts throughout all of his works, because he clearly
understood that it is necessary, first of all to advance
in Mental Sciences, to take the human being out of the
inertia and spiritual idleness in which he finds himself, which is all the Masters in the Inner Paths need
to convince him that he is endowed with superior abilities that he does not even suspect and that he can
put them at his service and at the service of all humanity. Atkinson also points out to us that the good or
bad use we make of our gifts and talents is what defi-
nes our whole morals, and that forces in themselves
are devoid of any qualities, being simply blind forces,

but receiving from our mind all the characteristics of good or evil. This author's point of view largely corroborates what Louis-Claude de Saint-Martin defended in his writings over a hundred years before the advent of New Thought. Note carefully these words of the Unknown Philosopher:

> *"It is by this will alone that the Principle, having become evil, originally gave birth to evil, and that it still perseveres there today: in a word, that it is by this same will that man has acquired and acquires every day this disastrous Science of evil, by which he sinks into darkness, while he was born only for good and for light."*
>
> THE UNKNOWN PHILOSOPHER
> IN "OF ERRORS AND TRUTH"
> COLLECTION "MARTINISM WITHOUT MYSTERIES"

Both authors affirm that man has a deep identity with the Light. However, he remains in a state of suffering for ignoring it or not knowing it, most of the time hindering the manifestation of that same Light by excessive attachment to the reality that is given to him only by his objective senses. All the miseries and uncertainties of this world are born from this limitation of his inner vision.

> *"We could describe the situation of the current man in a very childish way, but it will give us a clear vision between what he lives in this world and his true identity: man cries misery sitting on an infinite mine of gold and precious gems."*
>
> *S:: I::*

True wealth is already found within each one of us, and we don't have to go far to look for it, we just need to turn our gaze in the right direction: within ourselves. Contrary to what many people think, a social factor such as "poverty" is not a sine qua non condition for human beings to remain in this social state for their entire lives or to conform to it. Quite the contrary, it can be an aggregating element of power when the individual decides to use his WILL to fight against all the conditions that limit his expression on this material plane. The history of human civilization gives us countless examples of men who came out of the lowest social conditions and achieved enormous fortunes, all because of a mental attitude they assumed in front of themselves and the effort they made to overcome all their limitations and obstacles, training their mind and developing their innate superior talents.

William Walker Atkinson points out to us a fundamental reality that equals us as human beings, that we are all capable of great deeds as long as we WANT and educate our WILL to achieve our most precious dreams. Otherwise, our latent powers may lie dormant for a lifetime.

> *"It is always necessary to reinforce that external teachers, books, mystery schools are nothing more than facilitators of our task; not their executors. Therefore, there is no magic formula for coping with mental and spiritual laziness other than direct confrontation. The battle is within, and when we lose the war, it is never for vices but for our own weaknesses."*
>
> ***S:: I::***

All the great authors, versed in personal magnetism and mental influence, are unanimous when they defend the effort that each man must undertake to awaken his superior potentials in himself, since such gifts and talents are not acquired from outside, but developed from our inner world. Hence, the pressing need for effort and constant inner work, since our physical being is constantly interposed as an obstacle to inner perceptions, even though it serves as an armor for us to face the dangers that plague us in this world, in spite of all the corruption that this same material body imposes on us. And this the Unknown Philosopher reminds us in these words:

> *"If it were not possible for the man ever to recover the use of his strength, his chain would be for him neither a punishment nor a shame."*
>
> THE UNKNOWN PHILOSOPHER
> IN "OF ERRORS AND TRUTH"
> COLLECTION "MARTINISM WITHOUT MYSTERIES"

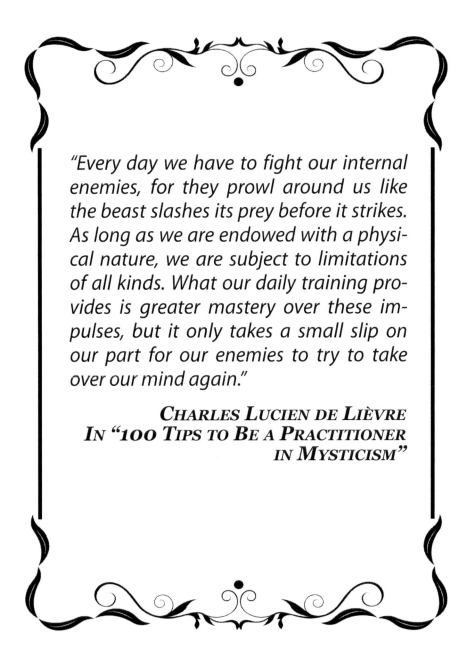

"Every day we have to fight our internal enemies, for they prowl around us like the beast slashes its prey before it strikes. As long as we are endowed with a physical nature, we are subject to limitations of all kinds. What our daily training provides is greater mastery over these impulses, but it only takes a small slip on our part for our enemies to try to take over our mind again."

CHARLES LUCIEN DE LIÈVRE
IN "100 TIPS TO BE A PRACTITIONER
IN MYSTICISM"

WHO WAS WILLIAM WALKER ATKINSON?

"Daily efforts towards inner development always bring good results, they only fail when they are not put into practice, either due to lack of trust in one's innate higher potentials, or due to physical or mental laziness. Anyway, you will find all limitations only in your being. Can you see the important role you play in your own inner growth?"

CHARLES LUCIEN DE LIÈVRE
IN "PHRASES OF IMPACT 1"

William Walker Atkinson (December 5, 1862 – November 22, 1932) was an attorney, merchant, publisher, and author, as well as an occultist and an American pioneer of the New Thought movement. He is the author of the pseudonymous works attributed to Theron Q. Dumont and Yogi Ramacharaka.

He wrote an estimated 100 books, all in the last 30 years of his life. He was mentioned in past editions of Who's Who in America, in Religious Leaders of America, and in similar publications. His works have remained in print more or less continuous since 1900.

LIFE AND CAREER

William Walker Atkinson was born in Baltimore, Maryland on December 5, 1862, to Emma and William

Atkinson. He began his working life as a grocer at 15 years old. He married Margret Foster Black of Beverly, New Jersey, in October 1889, and they had two children. Their first child died young. The second later married and had two daughters.

Atkinson pursued a business career from 1882 onwards and in 1894 he was admitted as an attorney to the Bar of Pennsylvania. While he gained much material success in his profession as a lawyer, the stress and over-strain eventually took its toll, and during this time he experienced a complete physical and mental breakdown, and financial disaster. He looked for healing and in the late 1880s he found it with New Thought, later attributing the restoration of his health, mental vigor and material prosperity to the application of this principles of New Thought.

∴

MENTAL SCIENCE AND NEW THOUGHT

Some time after healing, Atkinson began to write articles on the truths he felt he had discovered, which were then known as Mental Science. In 1889, an article by him "A Mental Science Catechism," appeared in Charles Filmore's new periodical, New Thought.

By the early 1890s, Chicago had become a major center for New Thought, mainly through the work of Emma Curtis Hopkins, and Atkinson decided to move there. Once in the city, he became an active promoter of the movement as an editor and author. He was responsible for publishing the magazines Suggestion (1900-1901), New Thought (1901-1905) and Advanced Thought (1906-1916). In 1900 Atkinson worked as an associate editor of Suggestion, a New Thought Journal, and wrote his first book, Thought-Force in Business and Everyday Life, being a series of lessons in personal magnetism, physic influence, thought-force, concentration, will-power, and practical mental science.

He then met Sydney Flower, a well-known New Thought publisher and businessman, and teamed up with him. In December, 1901 he assumed editorship of Flower's popular New Thought magazine, a post which he held until 1905. During these years he built for himself an enduring place in the hearts of its readers. Article after article flowed from his pen. Meanwhile, he also founded his own Psychic Club and the Atkinson School of Mental Science. Both were located in the same building as Flower's Psychic Research and New Thought Publishing Company.

Atkinson was a past president of the International New Thought Alliance.

PUBLISHING CAREER AND USE OF PSEUDONYMS

Throughout his subsequent career, Atkinson was thought to have written under many pseudonyms. It is not known whether he ever confirmed or denied authorship of these pseudonymous works, but all of the supposedly independent authors whose writings are now credited to Atkinson were linked to one another by virtue of the fact that their works were released by a series of publishing houses with shared addresses and they also wrote for a series of magazines with a shared roster of authors. Atkinson was the editor of all of those magazines and his pseudonyms authors acted first as contributors to the periodicals, and were then spun off into their own book-writing careers—with most of their books being released by Atkinson's own publishing houses.

One key to unraveling this tangled web of pseudonyms is found in "Advanced Thought" magazine, billed as "A Journal of The New Thought, Practical Psychology, Yogi Philosophy, Constructive Occultism, Metaphysical Healing, etc."

This magazine, edited by Atkinson, advertised articles by Atkinson and Theron Q. Dumont—the latter two were later credited to Atkinson—and it had the same address as The Yogi Publishing Society, which published the works attributed to Yogi Ramacharaka.

Advanced Thought magazine also carried articles by Swami Bhakta Vishita, but when it came for Vishita's writings to be collected in book form, they were not published by the Yogi Publishing Society. Instead they were published by the Advanced Thought Publishing Co., the same house that brought out the Theron Q. Dumont books—and published Advanced Thought.

HINDUISM AND YOGA

In the 1890s, Atkinson had become interested in Hinduism and after 1900 he developed a great deal effort to the diffusion of yoga and Oriental occultism in the West. It is unclear at this late date whether he actually ever subscribed to any form of Hindu religion, or merely wished to write on the subject.

According to unverifiable sources, while Atkinson was in Chicago at the World's Columbian Exposition in 1893, he met one Baba Bharata, a pupil of the late Indian mystic Yogi Ramacharaka (1799-c.1893). As the story goes, Bharata had become acquainted with Atkinson's writings after arriving in America, the two men shared similar ideas, and so they decided to collaborate. While editing New Thought magazine, it is claimed, Atkinson co-wrote with Bharata a series of books which they attribute to Bharata's teacher, Yogi Ramacharaka. This story cannot be verified and—like the "official" biography that falsely claimed Atkinson was an "English author"—it may be a fabrication.

No record exists in India of a Yogi Ramacharaka, nor is there evidence in America of the immigration of a Baba Bharata. Furthermore, although Atkinson may have traveled to Chicago to visit the 1892-1893 World's Columbian Exposition, where the authentic Indian yogi Swami Vivekananda attracted enthusiastic audiences, he is only known to have taken up residence in Chicago around 1900 and to have passed the Illinois Bar Examination in 1903.

Atkinson's claim to have an Indian co-author was not unusual among the New Thought and New Ages writers of his era. As Carl T. Jackson made clear in his 1975 article The New Thought Movement and the Nineteenth Century Discovery of Oriental Philosophy, Atkinson was not alone in embracing a vaguely exotic "orientalism" as a running theme in his writings, nor in crediting Hindus, Buddhists, or Sikhs with the possession of special knowledge and secret techniques of clairvoyance, spiritual development, sexual energy, health, or longevity.

The way had been paved in the mid to late 19th century by Paschal Beverly Randolph, who wrote in his books Eulis and Seership that he had been taught the mysteries of mirror scrying by the deposed Indian Maharajah Dalip Singh. Randolph was known for embroidering the truth when it came to his own autobiography (he claimed that his mother Flora Randolph, an African American woman from Virginia, who died when he was eleven years old, had been a foreign princess) but he was actually telling the truth—or something very close to it, according to his biographer John Patrick Deveney—when he said that he had met the

Maharajah in Europe and had learned from him the proper way to use both polished gemstones and Indian "bhattah mirrors" in divination.

In 1875, the year of Randolph's death, the Ukrainian-born Helena Petrovna Blavatsky founded the Theosophical Society, by means of which she spread the teachings of mysterious Himalayan enlightened yogis, the Masters of the Ancient Wisdom, and the doctrines of the Eastern Philosophy in general. After this pioneer work, some representatives from the known lineages of Indian and Asian spiritual and philosophical tradition like Vivekananda, Anagarika, Dharmapala, Paramahansa Yogananda, and others, started coming to the West.

In any case, with or without a co-author, Atkinson started writing a series of books under the name Yogi Ramacharaka in 1903, ultimately releasing more than a dozen titles under this pseudonym. The Ramacharaka books were published by the Yogi Publication Society in Chicago and reached more people than Atkinson's New Thought works did. In fact, all of his books on yoga are still in print today.

Atkinson apparently enjoyed the idea of writing as a Hindu so much that he created two more Indian personas, Swami Bhakta Vishita and Swami Panchadasi. Strangely, neither of these identities wrote on Hinduism. Their material was for the most part concerned with the arts of divination and mediumship, including "oriental" forms of clairvoyance and seership. Of the two, Swami Bhakta Vishita was by far the more popular, and with more than 30 titles to his credit, he eventually outsold even Yogi Ramarachaka.

∴

A French Master of Magnetism

During the 1910s, Atkinson put his attention into another pseudonym, that of Theron Q. Dumont. This entity was supposed to be French, and his works, written in English and published in Chicago, combined an interest in New Thought with ideas about the training of the will, memory enhancement, and personal magnetism.

Dual Career and Late Years

In 1903, the same year that he began his writing career as Yogi Ramacharaka, Atkinson was admitted to the Bar of Illinois. Perhaps it was a desire to protect his ongoing career as a lawyer that led him to adopt so many pseudonyms—but if so, he left no written account documenting such a motivation.

How much time Atkinson devoted to his law practice after moving to Chicago is unknown, but it is unlikely to have been a full-time career, given his amazing output during the next 15 years as a writer, editor, and publisher in the fields of New Thought, yoga, occultism, mediumship, divination, and personal success.

The high point of his prodigious capacity for production was reached in the late 1910s. In addition to writing and publishing a steady stream of books and pamphlets, Atkinson started writing articles for Elizabeth Towne's New Thought magazine Nautilus, as early as November 1912, while from 1916 to 1919, he simultaneously edited his own journal Advanced Thought. During this same period he also found time to assume the role of the honorary president of the International New Thought Alliance.

Among the last collaborators with whom Atkinson may have been associated was the mentalist C. Alexander, "The Crystal Seer", whose New Thought booklet of affirmative prayer "Personal Lessons, Codes, and Instructions for Members of the Crystal Silence League", published in Los Angeles during the 1920s, contained in its last page an advertisement for an extensive list of books by Atkinson, Dumont, Ramacharaka, Vishita, and Atkinsons's collaborator, the occultist W. de Laurence.

Atkinson died November 22, 1932 in Los Angeles, California at the age of 69.

WRITINGS

Atkinson was a prolific writer, and his many books achieved wide circulation among New Thought devotees and occult practitioners. He published under several pen names, including Magus Incognito, Theodore Sheldon, Theron Q. Dumont, Swami Panchadasi, Yogi Ramacharaka, Swami Bhakta Vishita, and probably other names not identified at present. He is also popularly held to be one (if not all) of the Three Initiates who anonymously authored The Kybalion, which certainly resembles Atkinson's other writings in style and subject matter. Atkinson's two co-authors in the latter venture, if they even existed, are unknown, but speculation often includes names like Mabel Collins, Michael Whitty, Paul Foster Case, and Harriett Case.

∴

A major collection of Atkinson's works is among the holdings of a Brazilian organization called Circulo de Estudos Ramacháraca. According to this group, Atkinson has been identified as the author or co-author (with individuals such as Edward E. Beals and Lauron William de Laurence of 105 separate titles. These can be broken down roughly into the following groups:

TITLES WRITTEN UNDER THE NAME WILLIAM WALKER ATKINSON

These works treat themes related to the mental world, occultism, divination, psychic reality, and mankind's nature. They constitute a basis for what Atkinson called "New Psychology" or "New Thought". Titles include "Thought Vibration" or the Law of Attraction in the Thought World, and Practical Psychomancy and Crystal Gazing: A Course of Lessons on the Psychic Phenomena of Distant Sensing, Clairvoyance, Psychometry, Crystal Gazing, etc.

Although most of the Atkinson titles were published by Atkinson's own Advanced Thought Publishing Company in Chicago, with English distribution by L. N. Fowler of London, England, at least a few of his books in the "New Psychology" series were published by Elizabeth Towne in Mount Holyoke, Massachusetts, and offered for sale in her New Thought magazine The Nautilus. On such title, for which Atkinson is credited as the author, with the copyright internally assigned to Towne, is The Psychology of Salesmanship, published in 1912. The probable reason that Atkinson made an assignment of copyright to Towne is that his "New Psychology" books had initially been serialized in Towne's magazine, where he was a freelance writer from 1912 at least through 1914.

TITLES WRITTEN UNDER PSEUDONYMS

These include Atkinson's teachings on Yoga and Oriental philosophy, as well as New Thought and occult titles. They were written in such a way as to form a course of practical instruction.

∴

When Atkinson wrote under the pseudonym Yogi Ramacharaka, he claimed to be a Hindu. As Ramacharaka, he helped to popularize Eastern concepts in America, with Yoga and a broadly-interpreted Hinduism being particular areas of focus. The works of Yogi Ramacharaka were published over the course of nearly ten years beginning in 1903. Some were originally issued as a series of lectures delivered at the frequency of one lesson per month. Additional material was issued at each interval in the form of supplementary text books.

Ramacharaka's Advanced Course in Yoga Philosophy and Oriental Occultism remains popular in some circles.

According to Atkinson's publisher, the Yogi Publication Society, some of these titles were inspired by a student of the "real" Yogi Ramacharaka, Baba Bharata, although there is no historical record that either of these individuals ever existed.

In reply to inquiries about Yogi Ramacharaka, this official information was provided by the Yogi Publication Society:

"Ramacharaka was born in India in about the year 1799. He set forth at an early age to educate himself and seek a better philosophy for living.

"Traveling throughout the East almost always on foot, he visited the depositories of books available. The primary places where libraries were open to him were lamaseries and monasteries, although with the passing of time some private libraries of royalty and wealthy families were also thrown open to him.

∴

"In about the year 1865, after many years of searching and many visits to the lonely high places where he could fast and meditate, Ramacharaka found a basis for his philosophy. At about this same time, he took as a pupil, Baba Bharata, who was the eight-year-old son of a Brahmin family. Together teacher and pupil retraced the steps of the teacher's earlier travels, while Ramacharaka indoctrinated the boy with his philosophy.

"In 1893, feeling that his life was drawing to a close, Ramacharaka sent his pupil forth to carry their beliefs to the new world. Arriving in Chicago where the World Columbian Exposition was in progress, Baba Bharata was an instant success. He lectured before enthusiastic audiences from all parts of the world who where visiting the Fair, attracting a considerable following in the process. Many wished him to start a new religion—but he felt only the drive to write on the subject which he lectured on so effectively.

"In the closing years of the 1800s, Baba Bharata became acquainted with William Walker Atkinson, an English author who had written along similar lines and whose had been published by ourselves and by our London connection, L. N. Fowler & Company Ltd.

"The men collaborated and with Bharata providing the material and Atkinson the writing talent, they wrote the books which they attributed to Yogi Ramacharaka as a measure of their respect. The very fact that after all these years their books are well known around the world and sell better with every passing year is a credit, too, to the two men who wrote the books."

Note that in at least one point, this "official" account is false: William Walker Atkinson was an American, not "an English author" and L. N. Fowler, an occult publishing house, was the British publisher of books that Atkinson had published under various of his own imprints in Chicago.

SWAMI BHAKTA VISHITA TITLES

Atkinson's second Hindu-sounding pseudonym, Swami Bhakta Vishita, billed as "The Hindoo Master" was not authentically Hindu, nor did he write on the topic of Hinduism. His best-known titles, which have remained in print for many years after entering the public domain, were "The Development of Seership: The Science of Knowing the Future; Hindoo and Oriental Methods" (1915), "Genuine Mediumship, or Invisible Powers," and "Can We Talk to Spirit Friends?" Atkinson produced more than two dozen Swami Bhakta Vishita books, plus a half-dozen saddle-stitched paper pamphlets under the Vishita name. All of them dealt with clairvoyance, mediumship, and the afterlife. Like Ramacharaka, Vishita was listed as a regular contributor to Atkinson's Advanced Thought magazine, but his books were published by the Advanced Thought Publishing Company, not by the Yogi Publication Society, which handled the Ramacharaka titles.

SWAMI PANCHADASI TITLES

Despite the popularity of his Yogi Ramacharaka and Swami Bhakta Vishita series, the work that Atkinson produced under his third Hindu-sounding pseudonym, Swami Panchadasi, failed to capture a wide general audience. The subject matter, Clairvoyance and Occult Powers, was not authentically Hindu, either.

∴

THERON Q. DUMONT TITLES

As Theron Q. Dumont, Atkinson stated on the title pages of his works that he was an "instructor on the Art and Science of Personal Magnetism, Paris, France"—a claim manifestly untrue, as he was an American living in the United States.

The Atkinson titles released under the Dumont name were primarily concerned with self-improvement and the development of mental will power and self-confidence. Among them were Practical Memory Training, The Art and Science of Personal Magnetism, The Power of Concentration, and The Advanced Course in Personal Magnetism: The Secrets of Mental Fascination, The Human Machine; Mastermind.

THEODORE SHELDON TITLES

The health and healing book, Vim Culture has often been attributed to William Walker Atkinson. Theodore Sheldon does not appear to be the same person as. T. J. Sheldon, who (like Atkinson) wrote on subjects related to health and healing for The Nautilus magazine and was also one of several honorary presidents of the International New Thought Alliance. Discovery of a 1925 letter from Theodore Sheldon to Florence Sabin of Johns Hopkins University provides evidence of Theodore Sheldon's existence as an actual person, apart from William Walker Atkinson. The original copy of this letter was located in Florence Sabin's university archives and makes reference to Ms. Sabin as Theodore Sheldon's childhood teacher from "the banks of Lake Geneva", which is important biographical data about an otherwise writer. While it's possible that Atkinson could have been a ghost writer or contributor to Sheldon's work, the personal nature of Sheldon's correspondence with Florence Sabin would have been very difficult for Atkinson to fabricate, suggesting that Theodore Sheldon was more than an Atkinson pen name.

MAGUS INCOGNITO TITLES

The Secret Doctrines of the Rosicrucians by Magus Incognito consisted of a nearly verbatim republication of portions of The Arcane Teachings, an anonymous work attributed to Atkinson (see below).

THREE INITIATES

Ostensibly written by "Three Initiates," The Kybalion was published by the Yogi Publication Society.

Whether any of the above has a basis in fact, The Kybalion bears notable structural resemblances to The Arcane Teachings, an anonymous set of six books attributed to Atkinson. A full description of the similarities between the two works can be found on the Kybalion page.

TITLES ATKINSON CO-AUTHORED

With Edward Beals, which may have been another pseudonym, Atkinson wrote the so-called "Personal Power Books"—a group of 12 titles on humanity's internal powers and how to use them. Titles include Faith Power: Your Inspirational Forces and Regenerative Power or Vital Rejuvenation. Due to the lack of information on Edwards Beals, many believe this is also a pseudonym.

With his fellow Chicago resident L. W. de Laurence he wrote Psychomancy and Crystal Gazing. L. W. de Laurence was an incredible character himself, publisher and author of dozen "occult" books that had a tremendous influence in many African and Caribbean countries, to the point that, they are banned in Jamaica.

THE ARCANE TEACHING' BOOKS

A series named "The Arcane Teaching" is also attributed to Atkinson. Perhaps significantly, the doctrine behind "The Arcane Teaching" is remarkably similar to the philosophy in "The Kybalion" (another title attributed to Atkinson), and significant portions of material from "The Arcane Teaching" were later re-worked, appearing nealy verbatim in the "The Secret Doctrines of the Rosicrucians" by Magus Incognito (yet another Atkinson alias).

Nothing is known of the first edition of "The Arcane Teaching", which apparently consisted of a single volume of the same name.

The second edition was expanded to include three "supplementary teachings" in pamphlet form. The four titles in this edition were: "The Arcane Teaching" (hardback), "The Arcane Formulas, or Mental Alchemy" (pamphlet), "The Mystery of Sex, or Sex Polarity" (pamphlet), and "Vril, or Vital Magnetism" (pamphlet). This edition was published by A. C. McClung—the same publisher who brought out the "Tarzan the Ape-Man" series by Edgar Rice Burroughs—under the "Arcane Book Concern" imprint, and the name of the publisher, A. C. McClung, doesn't actually appear anywhere upon the book in this edition. The series bears a 1909 copyright mark, listing the copyright holder as "Arcane Book Concern." There also appears to have been a pamphlet entitled "Free Sample Lesson" which was published under the "Arcane Book Concern" imprint, indicating that it may have appeared concurrently with this edition.

The third edition split the main title, "The Arcane Teaching", into three smaller volumes, bringing the total number of books in the series to six. This edition consisted of the following titles (the three titles marked with an asterisk (*) are the volumes that had appeared together as "The Arcane Teaching" in the previous edition): "The Only and the Many"* (hardback), "Cosmic Law"* (hardback), "The Psychic Planes"* (hardback), "The Arcane Formulas, or Mental Alchemy" (binding unknown), "The Mystery of Sex, or Sex Polarity" (binding unknown), and "Vril, or Vital Magnetism" (binding unknown) The third edition of "The Arcane Teaching" was published by A. C. McClung under its own name in 1911. The books in this series bear the original 1909 copyright, plus a 1911 copyright listing "Library Shelf" as the new copyright holder.

A search of the Library of Congress's web site has revealed that none of "The Arcane Teaching" series resides in its current collection.

∴

OTHER LIKELY PSEUDONYMS

Because Atkinson ran his own publishing companies, Advanced Thought Publishing and the Yogi Publication Society, and is known to have used an unusually large number of pseudonyms, other authors published by those companies may also have been pseudonyms;

A. Gould and Dr. Franklin L. Dubois (who co-wrote "The Science of Sex Regeneration circa 1912), and Frederick Vollrath (who contributed articles on the subject of "Mental Physical-Culture" to Atkinson's Advanced Thought magazine)

∴

O. Hashnu Hara. Although is hard to find concrete evidence, the first clue is always the impossibility to find information about the writer, other than the fact he wrote books published by Atkinson. Books under this name include: Practical Yoga; Concentration; and Mental Alchemy, all books with titles similar to other Atkinson's books.

BIBLIOGRAPHIES

For ease of study, this bibliography of the words of William Walker Atkinson is divided into sections based on the name Atkinson chose to place on the title page of each work cited.

BIBLIOGRAPHY OF ATKINSON WRITING AS WILLIAM WALKER (OR W. W.) ATKINSON

The Art of Expression and The Principles of Discourse. 1910.

The Art of Logical Thinking, 1909.

"Attainment with Honor", an article in "The Nautilus" magazine. June 1914.

The Crucible of Modern Thought. 1910.

Dynamic Thought or the Law of Vibrant Energy. 1906.

How to Read Human Nature: Its Inner States and Outer Forms. c.1918.

The Inner Consciousness: A Course of Lessons on the Inner Planes of the Mind, Intuition, Instinct, Automatic Meditation, and Other Wonderful Phases of Mental Phenomena, Chicago. 1908.

The Law of the New Thought: A Study of Fundamental Principles & Their Application. 1902.

The Mastery of Being: A Study of the Ultimate Principle of Reality & the Practical Application Thereof. 1911. A portion of this work was republished as a chapter of Pandeism: An Anthology in 2016.

Memory Culture: The Science of Observing, Remembering ans Recalling. 1903.

Memory: How to Develop, Train, and Use It. c.1909.

Mental Fascination. 1907.

"Mental Picture", an article in "The Nautilus" magazine. November 1912.

Mind and Body or Mental States and Physical Conditions, 1910.

Mind Building of a Child. 1911.

Mind Power: The Secret of Mental Magic, Advanced Thought Publishing Co., Chicago. 1912.

The New Psychology Its Message, Principles and Practice.1909.

New Thought: Its History and Principles or The Message of the New Thought, A Condensed History of Its Real Origin with Statement of Its Ba-

sic Principles and True Aims. 1915.

Nuggets of the New Thought. 1902.

Practical Mental Influence. 1908.

Practical Mind-Reading. 1907.

Practical New Thought: Several Things that Have Helped People. 1911.

Practical Psychomancy and Crystal Gazing, a course of lessons on the Psychic Phenomena of Distant Sensing, Clairvoyance, Psychometry, Crystal Gazing, etc. Advanced Thought Publishing Co. Masonic Temple, Chicago. 1907.

The Psychology of Salesmanship. 1912.

Reincarnation and the Law of Karma. 1908.

Scientific Parenthood. 1911.

The Secret of Mental Magic: A Course of Seven Lessons. 1907.

The Secret of Success. 1908.

Self-Healing by Thought Force. 1907.

A Series of Lessons in Personal Magnetism, Psychic Influence, Thought-force, Concentration, Will-Power, and Practical Mental Science. 1901.

The Subconscious and the Superconscious Plane of Mind. 1909.

Suggestion and Auto-Suggestion. 1915.

Telepathy: Its Theory, Facts, and Proof. 1910.

Thought-Culture or Practical Mental Training. 1909.

Thought-Force in Business and Everyday Life, Chicago. 1900.

Thought Vibration or the Law of Attraction in the Thought World, Chicago. 1906.

Your Mind and How to Use It: A Manual of Practical Psychology. 1911.

"How to Develop Perception", an article in "The Nautilus" magazine. July 1929.

The Seven Cosmic Laws, March 1931. (Published posthumously in 2011)

BIBLIOGRAPHY OF ATKINSON WRITING AS YOGI RAMA-CHARAKA

The Hindu-Yogi Science Of Breath (A Complete Manual of the Oriental Breathing Philosophy of Physical, Mental, Psychic and Spiritual Development). 1903.

Fourteen Lessons in Yogi Philosophy and Oriental Occultism. 1904.

Advanced Course in Yogi Philosophy and Oriental Occultism. 1905.

Hatha Yoga or the Yogi Philosophy of Physical Well-Being (With Numerous Exercises, etc.) 1904.

The Science of Psychic Healing. 1906.

Raja Yoga or Mental Development (A Series of Lessons in Raja Yoga). 1906.

Gnani Yoga (A Series of Lessons in Gnani Yoga). 1907.

The Inner Teachings of the Philosophies and Religions of India. 1909.
Mystic Christianity or The Teachings of the Master. 1908.
The Life Beyond Death. 1909.
The Practical Water Cure (As Practiced in India and Other Oriental Countries. 1909.
The Spirit of the Upanishads or the Aphorisms of the Wise. 1907.
Bhagavad Gita or The Message of the Master. 1907.

BIOGRAPHY OF ATKINSON WRITING AS SWAMI BHAKTA VISHITA

Can We Talk to Spirit Friends?
Clairvoyance and Kindred Phenomena
Clairvoyance: Past, Present and Future
Crystal Seeing by Seers of All Ages. (Pamphlet)
The Development of Seership: The Science of Knowing the Future; Hindoo and Oriental Methods. Advanced Thought Publishing Co. Chicago. 1915 (1 of 2 Actual Books)
The Difference Between a Seer and a Medium. (Pamphlet)
The Future Evolution of Humanity.
Genuine Mediumship or The Invisible Powers, Advanced Thought Publishing Co. Chicago. 1910 (1 of 2 Actual Books)
Ghost of the Living, End of the Dead.
The Great Universe Beyond and Immortality.
The Higher Being Develop by Seership.
Higher Spirit Manifestations.
How Is It Possible to Foretell the Future? (Pamphlet)
How Seership Develops a Constructive Life.
How to Attain Knowledge of the Higher Worlds.
How to Cross the Threshold of the Super World.
How to Develop Mediumship.
How to Develop Psychic Telepathy.
How to Distinguish Real Seership from Unreal. (Pamphlet)
How to Gain Personal Knowledge of the Higher Truths of Seership.
How to Go Into the Silence: The Key of All Life. (Pamphlet)
How to Interpret the Present and Future Exactly as They Are Designed to Be.
Mediumship.
Mental Vibration and Transmission.
The Mystic Sixth Sense.
Nature's Finer Forces.
Seership and the Spiritual Evolution of Man.

Seership, a Practical Guide to Those Who Aspire to Develop the Higher Senses.

Seership, the Science of Knowing the Future.

The Spiritual Laws Governing Seership.

Thought Transference.

What Determines a Man's Birth in a Certain Environment? (Pamphlet)

BIBLIOGRAPHY OF ATKINSON WRITING AS SWAMI PANCHADASI

Clairvoyance and Occult Powers. 1916.

The Human Aura: Astral Colors and Thought Forms. 1912. (Outlines his interpretation of the meaning of the various colors of the human aura)

The Astral World. Advanced Thought Publishing Co. Chicago. 1915.

BIBLIOGRAPHY OF ATKINSON WRITING AS THERON Q. DUMONT

The Art and Science of Personal Magnetism: The Secrets of Mental Fascination, Advanced Thought Publishing Co. Chicago. 1913.

The Advanced Course in Personal Magnetism: The Secrets of Mental Fascination. Advanced Thought Publishing Co. Chicago. 1914.

The Psychology of Personal Magnetism. (This version is copy of Advanced Course in Personal Magnetism)

The Master Mind or The Key to Mental Power Development and Efficiency.

Mental Therapeutics, or Just How to Heal Oneself and Others. Advanced Thought Publishing Co. Chicago. 1916.

The Power of Concentration. Advanced Thought Publishing Co. Chicago. 1918.

Practical Memory Training. Advanced Thought Publishing Co. Chicago.

The Solar Plexus or Abdominal Brain.

Successful Salesmanship.

The Human Machine. (Arnold Benett, not Atkinson)

BIBLIOGRAPHY OF THEODORE SHELDON (POSSIBLY AN ATKINSON PSEUDONYM)

Vim Culture.

Bibliography of "Three Initiates" (possibly an Atkinson pseudonym)

The Kybalion. Yogi Publication Society. 1908.

Bibliography of Atkinson writing as Magus Incognito

The Secret Doctrines of the Rosicrucians.

BIBLIOGRAPHY OF ATKINSON WRITING WITH CO-AUTHORS

W. W. Atkinson and Edward Beals, Personal Power Volume I: Personal Power

W. W. Atkinson and Edward Beals, Personal Power Volume II: Creative Power

W. W. Atkinson and Edward Beals, Personal Power Volume III: Desire Power

W. W. Atkinson and Edward Beals, Personal Power Volume VI: Faith Power: Your Inspirational Forces.

W. W. Atkinson and Edward Beals, Personal Power Volume V: Will Power

W. W. Atkinson and Edward Beals, Personal Power Volume VI: Subconscious Power

W. W. Atkinson and Edward Beals, Personal Power Volume VII: Spiritual Power

W. W. Atkinson and Edward Beals, Personal Power Volume VIII: Thought Power

W. W. Atkinson and Edward Beals, Personal Power Volume XI: Perceptive Power

W. W. Atkinson and Edward Beals, Personal Power Volume X: Reasoning Power

W. W. Atkinson and Edward Beals, Personal Power Volume XI: Character Power

W. W. Atkinson and Edward Beals, Personal Power Volume XII: Regenerative Power or Vital Rejuvenation.

W. W. Atkinson and L. W. de Laurence, Psychomancy and Crystal Gazing.

BIBLIOGRAPHY OF ANONYMOUS WORKS ATTRIBUTED TO ATKINSON

The Arcane Teachings. Chicago. n.p., n.d. [presumed 1st edition prior to 1909]; McClurg, 1909.

The Arcane Teachings: Free Sample Lesson, Chicago. McClurg, 1911.

The Arcane Formulas, or Mental Alchemy, Chicago. McClurg, 1909. McClung, 1911.

The Mystery of Sex, or Sex Polarity. Chicago, McClurg, 1909; McClung, 1911.

Vril, or Vital Magnestism The Secret Doctrine of Ancient Atlantis, Egypt, Chaldea, and Greece. Chicago. McClurg, 1909; McClurg, 1911.

The One and the Many. Chicago. McClurg, 1911.

Cosmic Law, Chicago. McClurg, 1911.

The Psychic Planes. Chicago, McClurg, 1911.

REFERENCES

1. Demetres P. Tryphonopoulos, The Celestial Tradition, p.66. Wilfrid Laurier University Press, 1992 – ISBN 978-0-88920-202-3.

2. *Works by Atkinson, William Walker 1862-1932 (WorldCat).*

3. *Works by Ramacharaka Yogi 1862-1932 (WorldCat).*

4. *William Walker Atkinson. Encyclopedia Of Occultism and Parapsychology, 5th ed. Gale Group, 2001.*

5. *Jackson, Carl T. (1975). "The New Thought Movement and the Nineteenth Century Discovery of Oriental Philosophy". The Journal of Popular Culture. IX (3) (3): 523-548. doi: 10.1111/j.0022-3840.1975.0903_523.x.*

6. *Deveney, John Patrick; Franklin Rosemont (1996). Paschal Beverly Randolph: A Nineteenth-Century Black American Spiritualist, Rosicrucian, and Sex Magician. State University of New York Press, ISBN 0-7914-3120-7.*

7. *"Author's Work", Circulo de Estudos Ramácharaca. Retrieved September 19, 2012.*

Source: *https://en.wikipedia.org/wiki/William_Walker_Atkinso*

WHAT YOU SHOULD KNOW BEFORE READING THIS BOOK

"The involuntary concentration is a thing to be avoided, for it is the allowing of the attention to escape the control of the will. The Mental Concentration of the occultists is a very different thing, and is solely in control of the will, being applied when desirable, and taken off or inhibited when desirable."

WILLIAM WALKER ATKINSON
IN "PRACTICAL MENTAL INFLUENCE"
COLLECTION "MENTAL SCIENCES IN PRACTICE"

1. Establish an individual program for your practical sessions and with well-defined and regular times. Our mind adapts to discipline because it acts like water that molds itself to the container that contains it. Therefore, impose your WILL on your impulses, as they will do anything to pull you out of your daily practices.

"The worst and most terrible demons are those that we create and cultivate even as traits of our character, for this reason they are very difficult to overcome due to the affection we nurture towards them."

S:: I::

2. It is much easier to focus your thoughts on external things than on your inner reality, as we are in the habit of projecting all our thoughts and desires to the outside world due to the strong conditioning imposed on us by our objective senses that makes us consider this material plane as our only reality. Even our highest spiritual aspirations are clothed in totally material aspects. For this reason, we have feel this strong difficulty to accurately perceiving our inner reality.

3. This inner reality manifests itself as long as we put our mental focus on it. In fact, it responds to the direct stimuli that we are able to give it, that's why a powerful mental concentration is so necessary. If you feel deprived of this faculty, you should do everything to develop it, because we all already have it, but it manifests itself in different degrees during the day and in a more intense or weak way depending on our interest. Therefore, develop an interest in your superior qualities, which will attract your attention, mental concentration, and the necessary action to develop your innate superior abilities.

4. Always keep in mind that the biggest enemies that prevent your success are inside you and are your creations. This factor is very important because it tells you that you can exercise power and control over them. Once you have mastered the power of these enemies through the application of your WILL, they become your greatest collaborators and a reserve of energy in your plexuses. So stop looking at temptations as something harmful to being, but on the contrary, take advantage of their energy making them work in your favor.

∴

5. Magnetic influence is a natural force in all human beings and, like concentration and other superior talents, manifests itself in degrees of expression more or less strong or weak according to the mental intention we dedicate to it and the actions we undertake for its development. In other words, we are all responsible for our greater or lesser success in life.

6. What the WILL is to the sage or the Magus, FAITH is to the common man. And what is WILL but CONSCIOUS FAITH? So have faith in yourself and your infinite potentials within. At the same time, take all the actions necessary for the development of your inner potentials, as they will not awaken on their own.

7. Read and reread this book and others in this series as carefully as possible, so that the theory about your inner powers, gifts, and talents is firmly fixed in your mind. However, and most important of all, practice the proposed exercises with determination, perseverance, self-confidence, so that as the results emerge, they will confirm the theory, increasing in an extraordinary way everything that has been exposed to you in these pages.

8. There are no shortcuts to success in life and in the Mental Sciences, except along the path of daily effort. Over time, effort turns to comfort, skill, and self-mastery. And all the tiredness generated and felt at the beginning of the exercises is transformed into pleasure and ecstasy of the soul.

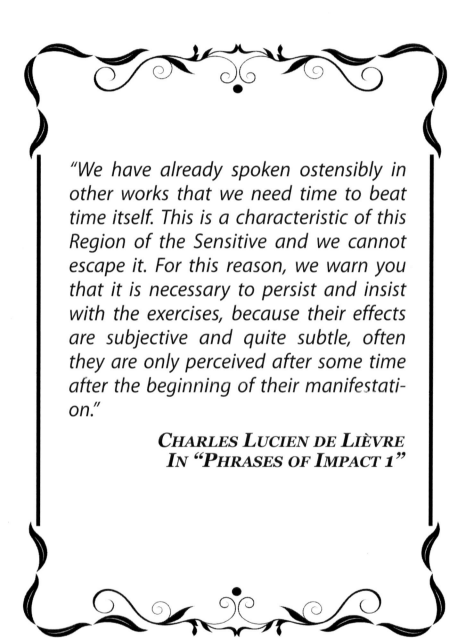

"We have already spoken ostensibly in other works that we need time to beat time itself. This is a characteristic of this Region of the Sensitive and we cannot escape it. For this reason, we warn you that it is necessary to persist and insist with the exercises, because their effects are subjective and quite subtle, often they are only perceived after some time after the beginning of their manifestation."

**CHARLES LUCIEN DE LIÈVRE
IN "PHRASES OF IMPACT 1"**

SPECIAL EXERCISES ON PERSONAL MAGNETISM

A set of three exercises to improve your personal magnetism to the highest grade, and with a detailed explanation on its benefits and obstacles. All exercises have been properly tested and proven in their benefits and obstacles, so they bring a detailed description of all their phases. Many of them were taught by William Walker Atkinson himself under his various pseudonyms.

"Practice associated with studies is the best path in terms of Mental Sciences, as experimentation always confirms the theoretical foundations of this science of man, which is a science of experimentation par excellence."

CHARLES LUCIEN DE LIÈVRE
IN "AWAKE THE GENIUS WITHIN YOU"
COLLECTION "MENTAL SCIENCES IN PRACTICE"

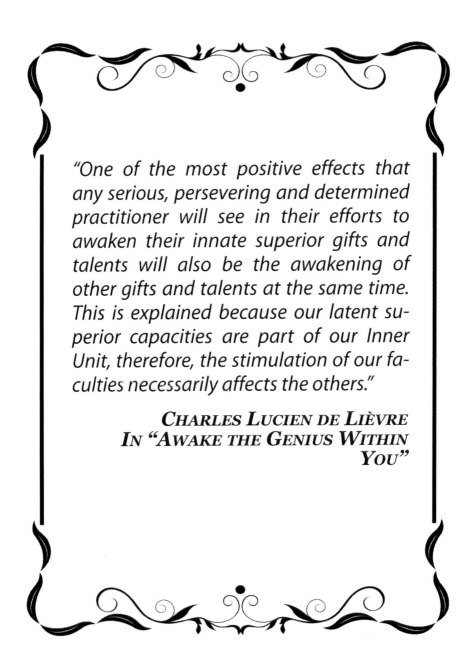

"One of the most positive effects that any serious, persevering and determined practitioner will see in their efforts to awaken their innate superior gifts and talents will also be the awakening of other gifts and talents at the same time. This is explained because our latent superior capacities are part of our Inner Unit, therefore, the stimulation of our faculties necessarily affects the others."

CHARLES LUCIEN DE LIÈVRE
IN "AWAKE THE GENIUS WITHIN YOU"

EXERCISE 1

CONCENTRATION ON BODY PARTS

"Dear reader, you will see us repeat this premise constantly and insistently: effort is the natural friction between the dynamism of the spirit and the slowness of matter. However, the predominance of either one or the other over our bodies and minds will always be a personal choice."

S:: I::

GOALS:

Putting voluntary attention on several different things by determination of our SOVEREIGN WILL.

Willingly shift thought to other parts of the body and amplify our personal magnetism and physical health.

Develop a high degree of voluntary concentration.

Control the flow of thoughts even with the shift in concentration.

EXERCISE DURATION:

The recommended time for this exercise is at least 1 hour and has no maximum time. Such time is recommended because the average psyche needs a time of 2 to 3 hours to be strengthened. That's why 1 hour should be considered as a relatively important time to overcome the resistance of the mind accustomed to indiscipline and lack of control over thoughts.

EXERCISE EXECUTION:

1. Sit comfortably in a straight-backed chair or arm-chair. Breathe slowly and deeply while mentally commanding your body to relax. Stay in this condition for about 15 minutes.

> IMPORTANT NOTE:
> You can also perform this exercise lying down if you are well rested or have practiced enough concentration exercises to allow you to have more control over your sleep.

2. When you feel quite calm and relaxed, focus on your feet as if they were the only parts of your body. Feel them starting with the soles, toes, heel. Allow your mind to run its full length. Visualize them with your eyes closed. If necessary, move them around a bit to focus your mental action on them even more. Stay focused on them for about 5 minutes.

3. Transfer your mind to your ankles and do the same as you did with your feet. Avoid any and all thoughts extraneous to the exercise. Concentrate on that part of the body as if it alone exists. Try to visualize the bones of the joints between the feet and the ankles. Let your mind penetrate inside. Feel the skin and flesh that envelop them. Stay with your mind focused on that region of the body for about 5 minutes.

∴

4. Now go up to the legs. Feel the shin bones, the muscles and the skin around them. Feel the touch of clothing or surroundings (if wearing shorts). Get involved with this thought and don't allow your mind to be invaded by thoughts that are extraneous to the exercise. The physical sensations you feel will allow you to keep your mind focused on those parts of the body.

5. Always repeating the same process, go up to the knees, after the stipulated time, go up to the thighs. Take your time. Bear in mind that a concentration exercise only achieves its effectiveness when attention is prolonged and maintained in the exercise. Now move up to the pelvis region, focusing on the base of the spine, the genitals and the internal organs of the lower abdomen. Keep your concentration there for the same recommended period. Feel the kidneys, the intestines, the bladder, the pelvis. Try to visualize them within you. If necessary, consult the images of these internal body parts on the internet to help visualize them.

6. Now raise the concentration to the navel region, trying to concentrate on the skin that surrounds the belly, on the back that is touching the back of the chair or armchair, on the part of the spine that is connected to this region. After the stipulated time, go up to the chest area. Focus on the central area of the chest and its inner part, feeling for the lungs. Focus on the ribs and the part of the back and spine that is at this height. Then concentrate for a longer time on the outer bone region, just below the heart. Remain focused on this region as you breathe through it.

7. Put the thought now on the entire arm of the hand you write with. Focus on your entire length, trying to feel all your muscles, skin, bones. Concentrate on the arm and hand until you feel the pulse along this part of your body. Then move to the other arm and repeat the same process.

8. Now transfer your mind and thoughts to the neck region. Try to feel all the muscles of the neck, the vertebrae that are part of it, the throat inside, the airways. Focus on trying to encompass the base of the neck evenly and concentrate for a longer or shorter period in this region.

9. Focus your thoughts now on the head region. Feel your entire skull, the bones of your face, the skin and the muscle that surrounds them. Feel the eyes in all their depth, the brain, the ears. Concentrate for a long time, running your mind through your head, feeling it both inside and out. Focus your thought on the area of the forehead that is between the two eyebrows and the root of the nose. After a while, transfer your thought to the region of the skull where the hair swirl is. Focus all your thinking on that region as well.

10. End the exercise and return to your normal activities.

Considerations On This Exercise

1. Upon completion of this exercise, you will feel a tremendous sense of well-being and physical regeneration. If you have more time, you can repeat the same exercise twice more in the sequence, always starting from the lower extremities of the body and going up to the head. You will double or triple the positive effects of this exercise.

2. The present exercise develops all the psychic centers (chakras) of our body, expanding our consciousness to other mental dimensions, in addition to the material effects already expected such as mental clarity, increased IQ degree, a powerful objective perception, increased creativity. It also promotes substantial strengthening of overall physical health.

3. It is a Raja Yoga exercise that should be made into a daily habit because of the limitless number of its benefits. Therefore, if there are owners of Truth requesting the possession of this exercise, know that, in addition to being a well-known practice of Indian yogis, it can also be found in many books and manuals on Raja Yoga and Kryia Yoga. The Truth does not belong to anyone, but it is a good of humanity and must be shared with everyone, as only those who are deeply inclined to them will be interested in these practices. Usually, those who defend the ownership of mysteries are the ones who practice them the least and do not want to see their own ignorance exposed. Hence their tendency to cover everything with the false veil of Mysteries more Mysterious than the Mystery itself. The point is quite simple: those who practice get effects, those who don't practice talk too much and flaunt unreachable Occult Mysteries!

> *"The great difficulty is always in convincing the human being to detach himself from the slavery of purely external perceptions and concentrate on his internal perceptions, therefore, speaking with erudition of the mystic is something very different than knowing it in practice".*
>
> ***S:: I::***

4. Therefore, dear reader, do not be another loudmouth full of theories of the property of the Mysteries and herald of the only true Knowledge, but be an example of experience and effective living of the Great Mysteries, because it is through your example that the people will be inspired, not through small talk and empty theories. Always keep in mind that "the word convinces, but the example drags".

5. Therefore, there is no way to separate theory from practice in the case of mental sciences. Otherwise, you run the risk of falling into charlatanism and the popular imagination that generate countless false beliefs and superstitions of all kinds. It is imperious that the mental sciences have their results, benefits and difficulties proven by individual experience.

EXERCISE 2

CONCENTRATION ON BREATHING

"The Law of Effort is a necessary and indispensable law on this Material Plane, since our physical being tends to pull us towards inertia due to its slower vibration. In order to impose the dynamism of the spirit on the slowness of matter, it is necessary to exert pressure on it, and this pressure is effort. No one is free from this law because it makes us recognize the duality of our nature."

S:: I::

GOALS:

Increase the flow of Prana or Essential Life Energy in the body.

Develop the psyche.

Substantially improve physical health, so as to avoid even colds and flu by increasing immune capacity and weather resistance. Increase concentration and develop the heart chakra by direct and sustained concentration on the chest.

EXERCISE DURATION:

This exercise is a variation of the previous one and can also be used as a preparation for other exercises due to its ability to produce physical and mental relaxation. Therefore, a minimum of 15 minutes and a maximum of 2 hours is indicated.

EXERCISE EXECUTION:

1. Like the previous exercise, this one can also be performed lying down as long as you are not too tired, otherwise you will be induced to sleep.

2. Sitting or lying down, focus on your chest area and feel your entire length, as well as your internal organs, your ribs, spine, back muscles and skin, lungs, and your heart. Concentrate on this part of the body as if there is only you and it in the entire Universe.

3. The physical sensation of touch and warmth increases in this region with concentration of thought; which makes it much easier to keep the mind fixed there. Put out of your mind any and all thoughts unrelated to the exercise. For this, forcefully impose your WILL.

4. Concentrate with all the strength of your being on your lungs as they are filled with air and also on your heart. Visualize that with each breath these organs are filled with light and are bathed in the highest currents of energy that renew them, make them more resilient and healthy.

5. Do the same procedure for the back and spine in that region. Feel that the ribs are also strengthened and renewed. Concentrate equally on the sternum (central chest bone) and repeat the same mental commands along with calm, peaceful breathing.

CONSIDERATIONS ON THIS EXERCISE

1. Calm and slow breathing greatly helps in suppressing depressive states and also eliminates anxiety. This exercise can also place our mind in a receptive state similar to hypnotic trance. It is in this state that the higher dimensions of the mind become accessible to the practitioner and through which one becomes able to perform certain miraculous feats similar to those practiced by the rishis (wise men of India), fakirs and western magi.

2. With a calm and more centered mind, in addition to deeper and not superficial breathing, there is a natural strengthening of health and an increase in immune resistance that prevent the emergence of flu and colds even in colder weather seasons.

3. Concentration maintained in the chest region naturally develops the psychic centers in this region of the body and promotes greater union between you and your Inner Master. Desire this union intensely, so that the influence of the limited ego is reduced on your personality and your Inner Self assumes its true position.

4. The slower and smoother your breathing, as well as deeper, the more the positive effects will be accentuated both on your physical health and on your psyche. In fact, there is a deep relationship between a high psyche and physical health, because only a high and balanced psyche is capable of guaranteeing a more permanent physical health.

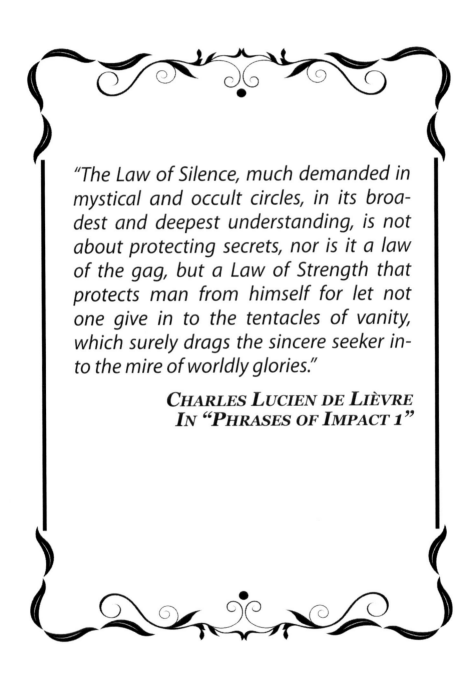

"The Law of Silence, much demanded in mystical and occult circles, in its broadest and deepest understanding, is not about protecting secrets, nor is it a law of the gag, but a Law of Strength that protects man from himself for let not one give in to the tentacles of vanity, which surely drags the sincere seeker into the mire of worldly glories."

CHARLES LUCIEN DE LIÈVRE
IN "PHRASES OF IMPACT 1"

EXERCISE 3

CONCENTRATION IN THE GLASS POT WITH WATER

"Note carefully that all the theory expounded in this practical method of personal development tends to convince the dear reader of the gigantic potentials that are enclosed in his being. This is the hardest part of any mastery: convincing the human being to break with their old beliefs and fully embrace their true inner identity, since no one can evolve in their place, nor can the best of all Masters take for themselves a task that only belong to us".

S:: I::

GOALS:

Powerfully develop the WILL.

Focusing thought on an external point.

Exercise self-control over the stream of thoughts.

Develop the magnetic gaze.

Apply autosuggestion formulas.

EXERCISE DURATION:

From 1 to 2 hours.

EXERCISE EXECUTION:

1. Take a pot, cup (glass or crystal). It can be a glass jar as long as the surface is smooth and very transparent. Choose one of these two containers and fill it with clean water.

2. Place this container on a piece of furniture at eye level. Make sure the wall behind the water container is free of objects or is a single color. You can fix a cloth or paper (dark color) behind the container as long as it is matte.

3. Cut some strips of white paper and write the following formulas for autosuggestion in very firm and large letters:

> *3.1 – MY WILL IS SOVEREIGN. I DOMINATE MY-SELF.*
>
> *3.2 – MY MENTAL CONCENTRATION IS INVINCIBLE AND EXTREMELY POWERFUL.*
>
> *3.3 – I AM LORD OF MY MIND AND MY THOUGHTS. I EXERCISE PERFECT DOMINION OVER THEM.*
>
> *3.4 – MY MIND IS STRONG AND MY CONCENTRATION IS POWERFUL.*

4. Write the sentences each on a slip of paper and choose one of them for the exercise for the first week of practice. Alternate the sentences each week.

5. Sit in a straight-backed chair, breathe slowly and deeply as you relax your entire body and clear your mind. Put away any and all thoughts unrelated to the exercise. Always have the phrase of the week at hand or within reach. Open your eyes and contemplate the sentence for about five minutes. Focus on its meaning and memorize the way it is written.

∴

6. Now look into the container of water and focus all your thought on the center of it. During this concentration, mentally visualize the autosuggestion formula inside the container of water. Mentally repeat the phrase to help with concentration. Use it just like a mantra.

7. Fix your mind for the stipulated period and don't allow your mind to wander. Every time it goes astray, forcefully enforce your WILL and bring it back. Remember that it is an exercise in self-mastery, and for that reason, inner confrontation through conscious effort will always be necessary.

8. When the exercise is over, throw the water out of the container and return to your daily activities.

CONSIDERATIONS ON THIS EXERCISE

1. This is one of the most powerful concentration exercises, however, one of the most difficult to perform, since keeping your eyes open and avoiding wandering thoughts is not so easy. However, practice generates aptitude and, over time, the initial difficulties turn into facilities.

2. Both the magnetic gaze as well as the projection of thought to the outside gain great power. It is an exercise that requires awareness and responsibility from the practitioner.

3. The SOVEREIGN WILL is powerfully stimulated, as the exercise brings together thought projection to the outside, autosuggestion and prolonged mental concentration.

4. Do not trust the detractors who claim that autosuggestion formulas do not work, as they base their opinions only on theories and are completely unaware of any form of practice. They are the "masters" and "great masters" of documents, cards and who live stuck in orders and initiatory schools that consider only their dead and empty rituals as the only form of spiritual ascent. Don't worry about them as they are defending their royalties and treasuries. They are not the least bit concerned with the effective practice of "Mystique" because it does not generate ratings, does not generate sycophants, in addition to worshipers of mediocre personalities, even because the real mystique cannot be "flaunted" nor registered in diplomas, much less paraded on the catwalks of vanity than today that many lodges have been transformed.

5. Be concerned with your inner work and trust yourself and those who have actual practice and experience, forget the small talk which are imposed with the sole desire to get personal adoration and slavish submission from the general public to the false adepts. Experience speaks more than a thousand books and those who know something effective convey what you need to know without fussing, pointing out all the difficulties along the way, because only those who have gone through the obstacles and felt the hardships of each practice are able to convey to you something really efficient and self-modifying. However, even the experience of great instructors will be null if you do not put yourself into action and abandon laziness and idleness. Therefore, work in silence and in retreat with the certainty that you will succeed, because the greatest of all Mysteries, the Holy of Holies, the Tabernacle of the Divine is on the Altar of your Heart. It is in this Temple that you must enter without hesitation, because it is in it that the true Threshold of the Mysteries is found.

6. The autosuggestion formulas work as messages of awakening to the Inner Self (Inner Master, Cosmic Christ, Higher Self) the name doesn't matter; what matters is the essence of the Ineffable Light that you already carry within you and it is up to you individually to awaken it, no one can do that for you. That's why we said at the beginning of this book that this is a non-transferable work. The auto-suggestion formulas described above were built on Cosmic Truths, Inner Truths, on a reality of which you are already the bearer, just awaken them in yourself. Therefore, such formulas are valid. But, you will have to find this out by your own experience.

7. No matter how wise and experienced the Master, no matter how traditional the School or Order you belong to, know that none of them can do this work for you. Just as none of them can quench your thirst or your hunger, or sleep for you. Mystical work has the exact same nature. It is up to you to do it, and you will only have as obstacles those that you impose on yourself, whether through laziness, negligence, abandon, inconstancy, impulsiveness or by constantly giving in to all the attractions of the external world. It is in the power of your WILL the force that will predominate in your destiny. The choice is always yours and no one else's.

> *"Don't be an idiot anymore who is playing at being part of mystical and initiatory schools, and playing at being a high initiate wearing ridiculous clothes that only inflate the ego with pride, arrogance, vanity and false pretensions. This attitude produces nothing but deception and disillusionment, as well as diverting you from the real mystical practice that can only be performed by yourself in the retreat and silence of your Individual Sanctuary."*

> *S:: I::*

8. The present exercise is extremely efficient and only those who have field experience can say that. Yet your WILL, your desire, will be constantly tested as in most of the exercises contained in this book. There will be times when you will think about giving up, when you will question if this is really what you want, if your desire is really sincere. This temptation is highly positive because it is part of the inner tests that you will have to overcome. It is the presence of "confrontation of yourself" as we have made clear in previous exercises. Know that this confrontation is part of your inner growth and you will have to go through it. It is the famous Threshold that you will have to cross, only this time for real, and not just on a symbolic level, as is done in most rituals in orders and initiatory schools. This is an effective key to your mystical asceticism. The "inner confrontation" is something direct, real, it does not remain on the symbolic level and should not be confused with it, because this struggle takes place within each one of us. And it's up to you to face the battle and win you.

9. No temple ritual, however elaborate, will not be able to describe this "inner struggle" until you make up your mind to go through it. There are no formulas for this, other than direct confrontation and real experience. After all, the battle is yours and you must take command of it.

PART 2

Containing the theory and practices as exposed by William Walker Atkinson.

"The great power of our soul is called WILL, and it is available to us all the time, that is, we can make use of this inner faculty at any day and at any time. In fact, it is this primitive right of man that forms the basis of what we call 'free will' and 'liberty'."

CHARLES LUCIEN DE LIÈVRE
IN "AWAKE THE GENIUS WITHIN YOU"

"The most learned occultists and the most experienced Mages are unanimous that all Magic is mental. It is man's thoughts that become a powerful magnet capable of influencing and attracting the Invisible Intelligences that inhabit other dimensions. Just as a magnetic man influences his audience, attracting to him more fame, sympathy and success, so does the Magus through his operations. The laws which operate in mental and magnetic influence are exactly the same as those which operate in any magical act."

**CHARLES LUCIEN DE LIÈVRE
IN "100 TIPS TO BE A PRACTITIONER
IN MYSTICISM"**

PRELIMINARY GREETING

I take pleasure in presenting to many American students who will acquire possession of copies of this book, these practical lessons on the art and science of Personal Magnetism. These chapters contain the gist of the lessons taught by me, in classes, and to individuals, in my courses of personal instruction conducted by me, here in Paris, for the past eighteen years.

In my personal class work, of course, I adapt the instruction to the special requirements of my individual students, which I cannot do in the case of general lessons in printed form. But, notwithstanding this, I feel that I have condensed into these pages the essence of my methods, and principles of practice, so that any student of average intelligence may readily grasp, assimilate, and apply the same with success, at least, I feel that if the student does not accomplish this, it will be his or her own fault, not that of myself.

In introducing this book, I wish to express my obligations to Mr. L. N. D., an American student of mine, here in Paris, who has kindly transformed my rather stilted "guidebook English" into the plain, simple form desirable for a book designed for the general public. I feel particularly indebted to him for supplying the idiomatic, American "man on the street" terms, thus reproducing the conversational style which I use in all my lessons in French, but which my "book in English" would render impossible in this case without the kindly assistance of this worthy gentleman.

With hand on heart, I send to my new American audience the sincere regards, and most earnest wishes for success, of

Their solicitous teacher,

THERON Q. DUMONT — *Paris, France, August 26, 1913*

CHAPTER 1

PERSONAL MAGNETISM

It is a strange and almost amusing fact that there should be at the same time, on the part of the general public, such a general acceptance of the existence of personal magnetism, on the one hand, and such an ignorance of the nature of this wonderful force, on the other hand. In short, while everyone believes in the existence of personal magnetism, scarcely anyone possesses knowledge of the real nature of the same, much less a working knowledge of its principles of application.

A belief in the existence of a personal power, influence, or atmosphere, on the part of certain individuals, which enables the possessor to attract, influence, dominate or control others, has been held by the race from the earliest days of written history. Many of the oldest writings of the race contain references to the strange, mysterious power possessed by certain individuals, which enabled them to attract or influence others. And, following the course of written human history along the ages, we may perceive a constant reference to this strange power of the individual, so generally acknowledged and at the same time, so little understood. Coming down to the present age, an age in which great attention has been devoted to the study of psychology and psychic subjects in general, we find that while the old belief in personal magnetism has been strengthened, there exists, at the same time, very little general knowledge among the public regarding the real nature of the force or the best means of using and employing it.

But this lack of knowledge just alluded too is confined to the general public. In all ages there have been a few advanced individuals who have thoroughly understood and employed the force of personal influence. Not only have the occult students of the past possessed this knowledge, and have passed it on to their successors, but many of the greatest men of history have acquired a thorough knowledge likewise, and have employed it in advancing their own interests. In some cases, individuals of this last mentioned class have received direct instruction from occult teachers, but in many cases they have stumbled across the existence of the power within themselves, and then advanced in their knowledge of the subject by careful investigation and study, accompanied by constant experimentation. Many of them, in their writings or sayings, have testified to their knowledge and us of this most wonderful power. It is difficult even to correctly define the term "personal magnetism," so little are its principles understood by the masses of the people. The dictionaries give us but little help in the matter, so vague are their so-called definitions. Perhaps the best definition is the following: "the strong, peculiar, but little understood power, force, or influence, exerted by certain individuals, in varying degrees, by the means of which other persons are attracted to, controlled by, dominated, or influenced by the individual possessing the power; a form of mental influence exerted by certain individuals over those with whom they come in contact."

The principal objection that I, personally, have to the above otherwise fairly good definition, is it implies that only certain individuals possess personal magnetism, the implication being that the remainder of the race are devoid of it. This, in my opinion, is a sad mistake. The truth is, each and every individual is in possession of a certain degree of personal magnetism; that each person may increase the degree and strengthen the power by knowledge and practice.

Even the most "non-magnetic" person possesses personal magnetism, perhaps even to a considerable degree, but is generally so ignorant of the nature of the force of the means of its employment, that he or she actually repels other persons instead of attracting them. For, do not fail to note this fact, personal magnetism, like material magnetism, may repel as well as attract — it has its positive as well as its negative side. Many very repellent persons are really manifesting a high degree of personal magnetism in a negative form, and are driving away persons from them in the same manner that others attract persons to them — it is all a matter of the use of the power.

∵

The fact is that every person generates and throws off a certain degree (varying among different individuals) of personal magnetism, which affects the minds of other persons coming within the field of its influence. Not only does each person emanate and project a certain amount or degree of personal magnetism, additionally, each person is also constantly surrounded by a field of personal magnetic influence — a personal atmosphere, so to speak. This personal atmosphere affects to a greater or lesser degree other persons coming within its field of influence.

This personal atmosphere varies greatly in degree of strength, extent and general character, among different individuals. The average person has but a weak personal atmosphere, which extends but a short distance on all sides of him, while the strong characters of the race are surrounded by a widely spread personal atmosphere of great, power, especially when they are aroused by any strong emotion, feeling or desire. The personal atmosphere of those strong individuals, who are generally recognized as leaders of the race, usually extends great distances from the person, and is fairly saturated with strong dynamic magnetism, which impresses itself strongly upon those coming within their field of influence.

∴

But even the weaker individuals of the race, or using personal magnetism unconsciously, exert at least some degree of influence upon those around them. It requires but a moment's thought to recognize that some persons emanate an atmosphere of good-cheer, brightness, and happiness, which affects in a desirable way all persons with whom they come in contact. Others, in the same way, are surrounded by an atmosphere of gloom, pessimism and discouragement, which adversely affects persons coming near them. These things are too common to even excite interest among the average persons, but in this phenomena may be found the key to the higher forms of personal magnetism.

We are so accustomed to regarding personal magnetism as meaning only the positive, attractive phase, that it comes as a shock to some of us to be told that the repelling personal atmosphere is equally "magnetic" – that is, magnetic in the wrong direction. This should cause no wonder, when we remember that even the physical metallic magnet repels, under some circumstances, as strongly as it attracts under others. There are, it is true, certain individuals who seem neither to attract nor repel, but this does not affect the general rule. These neutral individuals are usually of weak magnetism, and weak character – that is to say they have no strong motives, aims or desires, or strong cast of character or personality. Each faculty of the mentality is neutralized by some other faculty of equal strength, and the result is a neutral condition akin to lukewarm water- neither hot nor cold. It follows, naturally, that such persons exert but a neutral influence, and have but a weak neutral personal atmosphere. They neither attract nor repel – they simply "bore" persons with whom they come in contact.

∴

Some may raise the question that if, as I have said, each and every person is possessed of personal magnetism, then why should any one bother any more about the matter, or study the subject of personal magnetism at all. Such a question (and it is frequently raised, for that matter) causes a smile to manifest on the features of those who have knowledge of the subject; so childish does it seem to them. While it is true that each and every person is possessed of personal magnetism to some degree, it is equally true that the majority of persons have but a weak magnetic force, and that often of a negative or undesirable character. And, it is a fact positively known to those who have mastered the subject, that even the weakest and most negative person may so develop his or her personal magnetism as to gradually acquire the same degree and character of magnetism as that possessed by many individuals originally far in advance of them in magnetic influence.

One may completely change the character of his personal magnetism, from negative to positive, from undesirable to desirable, by careful study and practice along the lines, which I shall lay down in this book. Moreover, it is possible for any person possessing sufficient will, perseverance and determination to develop from a puny state of magnetism into a condition of giant magnetic powers. But this latter requires determination, constant practice until a certain stage is reached, and an indomitable will. While any one may easily increase his or her degree of power of personal magnetism, and still more easily change the character of one's personal atmosphere, the higher prizes are reserved for those who will persevere to the end, and continue faithful in the exercises. This, of course, is true not only of personal magnetism, but also of every other thing worth having. There is no royal road to anything worth having. We must work for what we get. The prizes are not for the weaklings and triflers, but for the persistent, earnest individuals who will "hang on" until they succeed.

In this little book, I give you the key to the secret of personal magnetism, but it will still remain for you, yourselves, to determine just what degree of success you shall attain. I give you the best tools, and instructions as to how to use them — but you will have to do the rest yourself. This I will say, however, success must and will be yours if you will follow the instructions carefully, persistently and perseveringly. That is all I can do for you — the rest is in your own hands.

CHAPTER 2

MENTAL AND PHYSICAL POLES

Some of the writers on the subject of personal magnetism have fallen into the error of considering that the entire secret of personal magnetism is to be found in the phenomena of telepathy or transference of thought. These writers, however, have been so carried away by the wonderful facts of the mental phase of personal magnetism, that they have entirely overlooked the other phase, i.e. the physical pole of the magnetic personality. This second phase is just as important as is the mental phase, and the person who wishes to cultivate and develop personal magnetism must give this second phase the same careful attention and practice as the first phase. There are two distinct phases or poles of personal magnetism, (1) the mental and (2) the physical. Do not fail to note this fact, for your success will depend upon the coordination of the force of both poles.

To many, this idea of there being a second or physical phase of personal magnetism will seem strange, so accustomed have they grown to hearing the teachings that personal magnetism is a mental phenomenon pure and simple. But as we proceed in our study of the subject in this book, I hope to thoroughly convince you that this second pole of personal magnetism really exists, and that it is equally potent as the first, or mental phase or pole. A man is a dual organism, with both mental and physical phases of manifestation, both mind and body, so is his personal force composed of two distinct phases or poles, each coordinating with the other in the work of manifesting energy and creating effects. Some persons have more mental magnetism, while others have more physical magnetism, but the individual who really manifests the highest degree of personal magnetism is the one who is developed along both poles of activity, both phases of magnetism — physical as well as mental.

The mental pole or phase of personal magnetism depends for its force and energy upon the ability of the mind to create thought-waves and to project them beyond the limits of the brain, into the personal atmosphere of the individual, and even beyond the range of his own personal atmosphere when necessary. When accompanied with the physical magnetism generated by the other pole of magnetic activity, this mental magnetism strongly affects other persons coming within the field of action of these thought-waves. But without a good supply of the physical magnetism, these thought-waves fail to have sufficient strength to produce marked results. It would seem that the physical magnetism were needed to give "body" to the mental magnetism, just as the mental magnetism is needed to give color, character or "soul" to the physical magnetism. The two phases of magnetism must work together to gain the best effects.

It was formerly very difficult to convey to the mind of the student the facts regarding the mental phase of personal magnetism, so strange did the whole thing appear to him. But in these days, when there has been so much written and taught regarding telepathy, thought-transference and mind-power, the average person is so well posted on the general subject that he may readily understand the special features of thought-power as manifested on personal magnetism. So it is not necessary, now, to first give the student a thorough education regarding the general subject of telepathy, in order to lead him up to the special subject of personal magnetism. In this book, I shall take it for granted that the student knows something of the subject of telepathy or thought-transference, and accordingly I shall not take up space and time in traveling over this old familiar ground. But, nevertheless, I think it advisable to point out to you some of the latest facts discovered by science in connection with the transference of thought.

Science has discovered that the human brain, in the processes of thinking, actually generates and uses up a certain amount of energy in the area of the brain tissue. The generation and employment of this energy produces heat, and actually increases the temperature of the brain areas, as may be proven by the use of the delicate registering instruments. Found in every well-equipped brain is as much an actual force as is electricity or the ordinary magnetism of the lodestone, and is governed by much the same general laws and rules. And, like electricity or ordinary magnetism, it is not confined to the point at which it is generated, but, instead, it may be, and is, diffused to points beyond. In other words, the thought energy of the brain of a person extends beyond the limits of his brain, creates a thought-atmosphere around him, and registers an effect upon the brains of others coming within his field of energy.

The discovery of radio-activity in certain newly discovered elements of matter, notably in the case of radium, has led science to investigate the matter of the possible radio-activity of other substances. The result is most surprising, for advanced science now announces that every substance is radioactive, that is, every substance is constantly radiating energy of force from itself. This discovery serves to harmonize the previously separated facts regarding thought-transference, etc., and it is now accepted as a fact that the human brain is strongly radioactive, and is constantly sending forth streams of radio-energy. The same laws, which govern the radium, are now perceived to govern the brain action. This simplifies the matter, and brings the subject of thought-transference into the general field of science, and out of the realms of mysticism. The subject is now taught and studied, on a scientific basis, in the principal universities of the world, and new discoveries are constantly being made regarding it. The physical pole of personal magnetism is not to be found in the flesh, blood, or bones of the body – for these are but the crude machinery by which the higher parts of the human organism moves and acts. Instead, it is to be found in that most wonderful part, or parts, of the organism, known as the nervous system. This nervous system is just as wonderful in its way as is the brain, and its effects in personal magnetism are just as important.

We are so apt to think of the nerves as being a part of the "body" of the person, that it is somewhat difficult for us to get the idea that the nervous system is really as much a part of the mental system as is the brain. In fact, the nervous system is composed of almost exactly the same kind of matter, as is the brain. The nervous system, moreover, generates energy of a kind very similar to that generated by the brain. For that matter, advanced science really considers that the brain and nervous system are but parts of one and the same thing, governed by the same general laws, and to be considered in connection with each other. And, the student of personal magnetism soon comes to accept this view, when he sees the important part played by the great nerve centers in the work of personal magnetism. Therefore, although I call the magnetism of the nervous system by the term "physical," and that of the brain by the term "mental," I do so merely in order to make an easy line of distinction for the purpose of teaching and study. At the last, however, they are really but parts of one and the same thing — merely two poles of the same source of energy.

∴

The nervous system of the human being is really a most intricate mechanism. Its main feature is the spinal cord which runs along an opening in the spinal column or backbone, and which is directly connected with the brain matter in the skull. From the spinal cord emerge many sets of nerves, in pairs, which branch out in smaller filament, these in turn branching out into still smaller, and so on, until each and every part of the body is supplied with a direct connection with the main nerve trunk. Other great cables of nerves descend into the trunk of the body, apart from the spinal cord system, although connected with the latter by nerve links. In different parts of the body are to be found great masses of nerve-substance, being matted knots or tangles of nerves, these centers being called plexus or plexuses, the principal one being the "solar plexus" which is situated right back of the pit of the stomach, and which plays a very important part in the life of the person, so important, indeed, that a severe blow struck directly over it may cause the death of the person.

The nervous system not only conveys messages from the different parts of the body to the brain, but also serves to convey the energy of motion to the various parts. In short, there can be no motion of any part of the body unless the impulse comes over the nerves. When the nerves governing any part of the body are paralyzed, that part of the body becomes devoid of motion. So you see, the nervous system is a part of the great energy-producing system of the body — as much a part of it as is the brain. Remember this, always, for it is one of the keys to the secrets of personal magnetism.

When you remember that this nerve-energy spreads itself beyond the limits of the body, just as does the energy of the brain, then you may begin to see what I am "driving at" in announcing the second pole or phase of personal magnetism, namely the "physical" pole, which, in reality, is the phase of magnetism generated and radiated by the nervous system, particularly by its great centers of plexus. I think that you are now beginning to get the idea, although I have carefully avoided technical scientific terms and have expressed myself in the simplest form.

CHAPTER 3

THE MENTAL PHASE

The mental phase of personal magnetism depends upon two coordinated manifestations of mental power, as follows:

(1) the holding of certain mental states until the mental atmosphere becomes charged with the vibrations of the particular mental states; and

(2) the conscious projection of the mental current from the brain centers, by the action of the will of the individual.

I shall now proceed to describe these two mental phases of manifestation in detail.

It is a fact known to all students of the subject that the character of the mental atmosphere of any individual depends entirely upon the character of the mental states held by him. The mental atmosphere of the hopeful, expectant individual is composed of vibrations of a hopeful, cheerful character, which tend to impress and affect other persons coming within the field of activity of his personal atmosphere. Likewise, the mental atmosphere of the gloomy, depressed individual is composed of vibrations of a gloomy, depressing character, which impresses and affects individuals coming in contact therewith. And, in the same manner, all of one's mental states will become manifest in his mental atmosphere, and accordingly, will affect those with whom he comes in close contact.

The truth of the above statements will become apparent to anyone who will give the matter a moment's careful consideration, remembering at the same time the impressions created upon him when he has come in contact with different individuals. He will remember that some individuals have left upon him the impression of gloom, inefficiency, failure, etc. Others have left with him a feeling of suspicion, distrust, and uneasiness. Others still have given him the impression of cheerfulness, friendliness, confidence, and good will.

The atmosphere of some persons is such that it causes us to let them alone, and to take no stock whatsoever in their business propositions. Others, instead, imbue us with confidence and trust, and give us the feeling that we would like to do business with them. Some persons leave upon us the impressions that we have been in the presence of a snaky thing, and we often can scarcely repress a shudder of disgust and dislike while others create in us the impression that the other person is a good friend and can be depended upon as a helper and comrade. Why?

It is not from anything these persons have said, for, as we all know, some of the slipperiest persons are often the best and smoothest talkers; and some of the best and most dependable persons are often very reticent, and even "short" in speech. The reason lies deeper that words. It is the "feeling" that we experience when we come in contact with persons, rather than any report of the reason regarding them. And this "feeling" is caused by the registry upon our sensitive brain organism of the thought-vibrations of the other person's personal atmosphere. Not only are these things noticed in the person himself or herself, but even the very residences, stores or other places frequented by the individual are also affected by the continuous influence of the thought-vibrations of his or her personal atmosphere. Did you ever notice how some houses produce upon you a feeling of sadness or woe, or worse; while others seem to carry within them an air of health and good cheer, happiness and content? This is often true although the house may have been unoccupied for some time. So strong do the mental vibrations of the atmosphere of the person or persons formerly inhabiting them. In the same way some offices and places of business are so saturated with the vibrations of the personal atmospheres of their occupants, that one is forcibly impressed by the same upon entering the door. A man may disguise his thoughts by his words or his facial expression, but the mental vibrations of his personal atmosphere will frequently "give him away."

∴

These are facts, which should require no further proof — your own experience should be proof enough to satisfy you but you should make mental note of this fact, and carry it in mind as we proceed. Many persons leave but little impression upon us, for the reasons that their mental states are so varied, inconstant and fleeting that they neutralize each other, and fail to impart a definite shade of thought-color to the personal atmosphere. The strongest personal atmospheres are those of persons of strong feelings, desires and emotions, good or bad, for such have strong and constant mental states which impress themselves forcibly upon their personal atmosphere, so strongly, in fact, that one who notices these things cannot fail to perceive them.

A moment of thought will inform you that if these things are true — and true you will realize they must be when you give the matter a moments' careful thought — then one should be very careful to avoid harboring mental states of a character likely to inspire undesirable feelings in other persons. And, at the same time, one should endeavor to cultivate mental states of a character likely to awaken feelings of a desirable character in those with whom we come in contact. In fact, a great portion of the following chapters will be used to teach how to cultivate just such mental states so as to rate the desired effect upon others, for in this lies one of the great secrets of personal magnetism.

∵

One need not despair if he has been creating and carrying around with him a personal atmosphere of an undesirable kind. For these things may be remedied, and one may entirely change the character of his mental states, and thus transform his personal atmosphere from the very worst to the very best. These things require work, perseverance, and patience, it is true, but the reward is so great that it pays anyone to devote his attentions and time to it. The principle is very simple, indeed, but it requires determination and dogged will to obtain the best results, particularly in cases where very undesirable conditions have existed.

The second way in which the mental phase of personal magnetism operates, i.e., that of the conscious projection of the mental currents from the brain centers, by the action of the will of the individual, also demands work on the part of the student who wish to create a strong personal atmosphere.

The principle of this second form of mental action consists in the use of the will in a conscious projection of thought-currents. This is true in the case of stimulating the personal atmosphere, and also in cases in which one endeavors to produce an effect upon the mind of some other person in whose presence he may happen to be.

While it is true that the character of the mental states of the person will color and give character to his personal atmosphere, which will, of course, produce an effect upon the other person or persons in his field of action, it is likewise true that the effect of such mental vibrations may be enormously increased by the use of the will in the direction of the conscious projection just referred to. The mental states produce and create the mental atmosphere, it is true, but the will serves to project them forth with force, and to generally energize the atmosphere and increase the effect.

∴

It is just as if you had created a great store of mental magnetism in your brain, and given it the proper quality and color by the character of your mental states. This would naturally create a personal atmosphere or aura around you, which would be felt by others. But then imagine the increased strength and effect that would arise from the use of your will to project and force outward from your brain these mental vibrations. You will see at once how such an action of the will would tend to energize and increase the vibrations of your mental atmosphere, can you not? It would be like turning on an extra force of the power, would it not? Certainly it would, and you may gain this effect whenever you wish to do so, by using the methods, which will be given you in this book as we proceed.

Again, you will see, by a little thought, how much stronger will be the effect upon any special individual, if, in addition to the vibrations of our personal atmosphere, we add the force of a special current of mental force directed steadily and pointedly at his mind, by an effort of our will. Do you see the point? You first affect him by the effect of your energized personal atmosphere, and then just when he is in the proper receptive condition you discharge at him a psychic rifle-ball which hits him right in the bull's eye of his mind with enormous force.

At first thought, this may seem to you like very strenuous proceedings, and one which would require the outlay of a great amount of will power on your own part. But, this is not so, for the thought-currents are very responsive to the action of the will, and the main thing is to hold the will firmly to the task, and the thought-currents will flow out over the channel thus made for them. It is like holding a rifle properly aimed, and then letting the force of the powder drive the bullet home; or, again, like holding the nozzle of a hose pointed exactly where you wish the current of water to go, and lo! When the water is turned on, it flies straight to the mark, long after it has left the tip of the nozzle of the hose.

The strong men of all times have employed the will in this way in the direction of creating a strong personal atmosphere, and also in the direction of producing strong impressions upon those who they wished to affect. In many cases they have not fully understood the character of the forces set into operation by themselves, but they understood the "how" part, even if they did not grasp the "why". The next time you come into contact with a strong individual, watch him or her, and see if you cannot almost see the operation of this direction of mental force of which I have just spoken. But, far more important than even studying others, is that of cultivating the art of doing the thing for yourself, and this is what I am trying to teach you to do. And you will succeed in it, too, if you will enter into the work fully with heart and mind. Get in earnest about it, and the power will develop in you to bring about success.

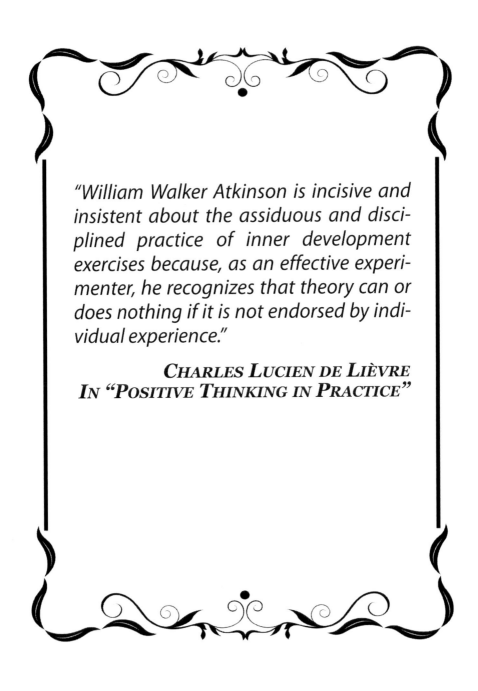

"William Walker Atkinson is incisive and insistent about the assiduous and disciplined practice of inner development exercises because, as an effective experimenter, he recognizes that theory can or does nothing if it is not endorsed by individual experience."

CHARLES LUCIEN DE LIÈVRE
IN "POSITIVE THINKING IN PRACTICE"

CHAPTER 4

THE PHYSICAL PHASE

The physical phase of personal magnetism depends upon two coordinated manifestations of nerve-force, as follow:

(1) the generation within the nervous system of a plenteous supply of nerve-force; and

(2) the conscious projection, by the will, of that supply of nerve-force into the personal atmosphere, and even to a greater distance under special conditions.

By "nerve-force," as used in the above paragraph, I mean that strange, mysterious form of energy, which controls all physical movements, and yet, at the same time, appears to be something higher than physical itself. It is akin to electricity or magnetism, in its real nature, and, like these forces is impossible to define. Nerve-force is something far different from the matter of which the nervous system is composed. The nervous system, from spinal cord to the most delicate nerve filament, is at the best but a system of wires, relays, etc., over which the nerve-force travels, or, else complicated reservoirs in which the nerve-force is stored.

The ordinary nerves serve as wires and cables over which the nerve-force travels to move the parts of the body, which we will to move, or which our subconscious mentality desires to move. Certain parts of the brain are great reservoirs of nerve-force, as are also the great groups of nerve-matter called the plexus, prominent among which are the solar plexus, and the sacral plexus.

The ordinary textbooks of physiology pass over the question of the real nature of nerve-force, for their writers do not possess the secret. They dispose of the question by saying: "As in the case of electricity, while we fully recognize its existence and its power, nevertheless we do not know its real nature." And, so, the student must go back to some of the old occult writers of the past ages, and their followers in the present age, in order to get the secret.

All occultists, ancient and modern, have recognized the existence of a mighty subtle force of nature — one of nature's "finer forces" — which is most potent it its effects and activities, but which, nevertheless, defied all power of analysis or definition. The reason that science has never been able to classify nerve-force is because, like electricity, it is in a class by itself, and is different from any other form of force — so different that it cannot be classified with other forces. Science, in some cases, has endeavored to treat it as a secretion of the nervous matter, but that is a folly akin to that of the materialistic philosopher who tried to define mind as "a secretion of the brain," just as the bile is a secretion of the liver, the gall a secretion of the gall-bladder, etc. Such attempts at definition cause only a smile on the face of the wise.

∴

The occultists, on the contrary, while not attempting to define nerve-force (recognizing it to be in a class of its own) nevertheless have discovered the source of its origin, and have given us valuable information as to its use. They have given it many names, as for instance: "vital force," "vital energy," "life force," "vital fluid," "vital magnetism," etc., and in the case of the Orientals, the terms "prana," or "akashic energy" have been applied to it. But under all of these different names, the occultists have always meant the one and same thing, i.e., nerve-force. The name I use in describing it, "nerve-force," is employed simply because it is found specialized in the nervous system, and not because of any idea that it originates there. Indeed, as you shall see in a moment, it has a far higher and more elementary source of origin.

The old materialistic school of physiology has attempted to show that nerve-force, like the bodily material, is derived from the food we eat, and is created by chemical combustion of the latter. This, however, is only partly true. While it is true that there is a certain amount of nerve-force in fresh food (having been gathered there during the life of the plant of animal of which the food formed a part), and while it is true that a certain amount of this nerve-force is taken up by the system of the person eating the food, particularly if the food be fresh, nevertheless, the amount of nerve-force so absorbed is comparatively small, and is far too little to supply what is needed by the individual to run his physical organism. And, even the small part so obtained is not derived from the chemical combustion of the food. Food chemical combustion results in giving bodily heat, but never in creating nerve-force.

The true source of nerve-force is the same as the source of electricity, namely the universal ether that fills space. Like electricity, also, this force is available to human wants only when it is associated with. The atmosphere is charged with nerve-force, which is taken up and absorbed by the nervous system, and stored away in its great reservoirs, from whence, in turn, it flows over the nerves when required, by the physical or mental needs of the individual.

But, you naturally ask, how does the body absorb the universal nerve-force — through what channel does it enter the system. The answer is plain, viz.: In plant, animal, and human life, the nerve force is breathed into the system. In other words, the process of breathing, in its higher and lower forms, is not alone that of extracting oxygen or other elements from the air, but also that of extracting the universal nerve-force at the same time. When this is understood, it will be more easily understood why the living thing perishes so soon if the process of breathing be interfered with. The understanding of this secret of nature throws a much-needed light upon the important part played by breathing, in the life of all creatures.

Before proceeding to a further consideration of the process of the absorption of nerve-force from the atmosphere, especially in the case of the student of personal magnetism, I ask you to consider another important question in relation to the physical phase of personal magnetism, namely, that of the projection of nerve-force beyond the limits of the nervous system. You will remember that the average physiologist maintains that it is folly to hold that nerve-force can possibly pass beyond the limits of the nervous system containing it. He holds that, like electricity on the wires, it cannot pass except over the wires of the nerves. But, is this true even of electricity? I positively assert that it is not. The veriest novice in the study of electricity is aware that electricity will often leap from one conducting substance to another — jumping the gap in the shape of a spark — and then flying along the new channel. Again, even without the spark, electricity and magnetism will often affect other substances by what is known as "induction," without the actual contact of the two conducting materials. This is so common that it is a wonder that the question is ever raised. And, what is true of electricity and magnetism, in this respect, is likewise true of nerve-force, for it will not only often leap over the barriers of the nervous system, but will, and constantly does, affect other nervous systems by a kind of "induction."

Not only is the phenomena of personal magnetism a proof of this transmission of nerve-force, but the phenomena of "human magnetism" (as it has been called) in the direction of "magnetic healing" another proof — a proof, moreover, that may be obtained by any individual in his own experience.

Moreover, the experience of every individual will bear ample and generous testimony to the fact that certain persons, flowing over with vigorous nerve-force, will so radiate the energy that it is actually perceptible to those shaking hands with them, or even coming into their vicinity. These individuals fairly radiate health and vigor, and exert a positive healing and invigorating effect, on those with whom they come in contact. In a similar manner, is manifested a lack of sufficient nerve-force, by those unfortunate individuals who go around unconsciously absorbing the nerve-force of others, and, in extreme cases, becoming actual vampires sucking the vital forces from those around them. Who of you have not met this last class of persons, and have not noted how depressed and weakened one is after having been in the company of such persons for some time? The average person does not need any further proof in this case, beyond that afforded by his or her own experience.

It may be asked that if the nerve-force is inherent in the universal ether, and obtained from the atmosphere, why all persons are not equally endowed with this energy. The answer is that the life-habits of individuals differ, and just as one is physically strong and robust, and another weak and delicate, so is one individual strong in nerve-force, and another weak in it. Moreover, a change in the life habits of the person will inevitably result in a change in the amount of nerve-force absorbed and retained by him or her. In fact, one of the purposes of this book is to instruct you how you may increase the nerve-force within yourself. While the object is the increase of your personal magnetism, you will find that at the same time your general health and vigor will improve.

In addition to the amount of nerve-force being determined by the life habits of the individual, it is also true that the individual may, by the proper exercises, so "energize" his nervous system that he will largely increase the degree of activity of his nerve-force, and may render it far more available for his requirements. It isn't only a question of securing a plenteous supply of nerve-force, but also of having the same in an active condition, and in such a form that it may be readily available for the requirements of everyday life.

CHAPTER 5

PHYSICAL MAGNETISM

You will remember that when you have come in contact with any of the strong characters in any walk of life — the great preachers, lawyers, statesmen, orators, businessmen, etc. — those whose success depends upon the strong effect they produce upon other persons, — you have been conscious of a feeling that they radiate strength and power. You actually felt the power coming from them. And, you will also remember that this power did not seem to you to be mental power, or intellectual strength, alone — it seemed, instead, to have much of the physical in it. So strong is this power in the case of some of the world's great characters that they seem to be personified will power — mighty centers of vitalized energy, affecting all with whom they come in contact.

In order to realize the difference between this power and pure intellectual strength and ability, you have but to remember another class of gifted persons, namely, the great students, writers, etc., and other men who have developed great intellectual power. These men as a rule are not "magnetic," as the term is generally used. They do not radiate or throw off force, and the element of physical magnetism is almost entirely absent. They seem to be centers of great intellectual energy — but nothing more. I am not now speaking of individuals in whom both the intellectual and the physical are well balanced and combined, but instead, of those individuals who are distinctly "mental" or intellectual. A moment's thought will recall many examples of the type to which I refer — the teachers, preachers, lawyers, and students whose intellectuality is well developed, but who lack that "something" which impresses persons.

Another appeal to your memory will show you; also, that the "magnetic" person is almost always possessed of that indefinable something, which we call "strength" and energy. He may not be a stout, large person — he may even be a scrawny, lank individual, of slight frame and small stature — but even in the last case he will be "wiry" and like a coiled wire spring, full of latent energy. The magnetic person is never the weak, flabby, jellyfish type. I have seen these thin magnetic persons on their deathbeds, weakened by disease, but even in their last moments they gave one the impression of keen spring-like strength. The other type of magnetic person, the stout type, also gives the impression of power and strength — a something within which stores and radiates strength and power. Is this not so in your own experience? Did you ever see a great leader — a magnetic personality — who did not convey the idea of "strength" in the physical sense? I think not.

Now, remember, that I am not claiming that physical nerve-force alone constitutes personal magnetism. Far from this — there are many men who possess and radiate physical nerve-force who are not personally magnetic in the full sense of the term. The combination of mental magnetism, and physical magnetism is needed to produce the full phenomenon of personal magnetism, remember. But, I do insist that mental magnetism without its physical counterpart is like a mind without a body – it lacks substance and effectiveness.

The occultists inform us that in the personal atmosphere of the individual — his "aura," they call it — there is to be found not only the vibrations of his mental states and character, but also the vibrations of his physical magnetism, or nerve-force as I have called it in this book. They state that to those who have developed psychic or clairvoyant power, these nerve-force vibrations may be seen extending from the body some two or three feet in either direction, the whole aura having an egg-shape, hence its name. It is said to have a faint violet color — something like a pale electric flame — and to quiver and vibrate in a manner similar to the motions of heated air arising from a stove, or the ground on a hot summer day, so familiar to every observer. They also claim that when a strong person is using his will, this nerve-force, carrying with it his mental magnetism, may be seen shooting in great sheets or flashes from him to the other person or persons. I do not claim to posses this psychic vision myself, but the testimony of many of my psychic friends agree in this matter, and are in accord with the writing of the older occultists. And, at any rate, anyone experimenting with personal magnetism will be convinced that nerve-force or physical magnetism does act in just the way described, though it remains unseen by the eye of the ordinary person.

Another important bit of information furnished by the occultists which is fully verified by my own observations and experiments, and which in fact forms one of the foundation pillars of my system of personal magnetism, is that concerning the part played by nerve-force in the phenomena of telepathy, hypnotism, mental influence, and similar phenomena in which the mind of one person acts upon the mind of another — this of course being one of the main features of personal magnetism. I allude to what may be called the "vitalizing" of the thought-waves by the current of nerve-force, which is projected at the same time with it.

Thought-waves unaccompanied by currents of nerve-force lack force and effect, and are like cold mental power devoid of life and activity. You will grasp this idea better by reference to a common occurrence, for instance, you have heard many a sermon, speech, or recitation delivered by a person having marked intellectual ability, and filled with good sound thoughts, — and yet the delivery seemed dead, dull, colorless and lifeless, did it not? It lacked the life, vigor, and vim of the delivery of some other speaker of even less intellectual power, did it not? And, you have noticed that the personality of some admittedly intellectual personage lacked "life"; while some other less gifted personality fairly radiated life and strength, and consequently, magnetic power. Well, this represents the difference between plain thought-waves, and thought-waves accompanied by strong nerve-force. The one lacks "body" and vitalizing force, while the other possesses this in abundance. Think over this carefully, until you "get it" — for in it lays one of the two great secrets of personal magnetism.

A person in whom nerve-force is actively present, and who has consciously or unconsciously acquired the art of combining it with his thought-waves, will send forth words or thoughts fairly charged with dynamic force, reaching and affecting those with whom they come in contact. Like a high-power explosive shell, the nerve-force drives the thought-wave like a bullet to this mark, hitting the bull's eye with a tremendous impact, and making a powerful impression on the mind of the other person or persons. There are persons whose words seem fairly alive, so vital is their action upon the minds of others — these persons have strongly active nerve-force or physical magnetism used in connection with their mental currents. They flash out this combined force toward their audiences of many persons, and the latter are fairly lifted off their feet by the power.

The great leaders of men have had this nerve-force largely developed and actively employed. When they spoke, the other persons were almost compelled to do the bidding of the strong person. Julius Caesar and Napoleon Bonaparte were two marked examples of the use of this power, but, as a fact, every man who sways moves and rules other persons, is an example worthy of study. The student should, if possible, manage to be thrown in contact with this class of persons, so that he may see, or rather feel, for himself, the effect of this mighty force emanating from these individuals. He will then better realize just what part nerve-force plays in the matter of personal influence, and personal magnetism, and then be more firmly resolved to develop it in himself or herself.

There are some persons who seem, naturally, to absorb, store up and effectively use their nerve-force of physical magnetism. Such are very fortunate, for they are saved the trouble of cultivating the processes referred to. But those who do not possess this gift, naturally, may by practice and perseverance develop it in themselves. Nay, more, they may, eventually, even surpass the naturally-gifted man, for the latter does not understand the source or nature of his power, and

is apt to neglect or abuse it, while the person who develops it in himself, according to rule, and with a full
understanding, has the thing "on tap" as it were, and
can always recuperate from an over drain on a nervous
system. Knowledge is power, and a cultivated and developed faculty is often far more effective than a similar faculty present at birth, and not understood or
worked for.

Beginning with the next chapter, I purpose giving
you plain, simple directions for the increase of your
nerve-force, the storing up of the same, and the conscious projection of it to vitalize your mental currents.
The process is quite natural, and does not partake of
any mystic ceremonies or anything of that sort. It is
based on purely physiological principles, and is in full
accord with natural laws. When you have once acquired the art and science of the absorption and storing of
nerve-force, you will be surprised that you have never
thought of it before.

When you acquire this power, you will be conscious
of being a center of an enormous energy, and will also
be made aware of your power by the effect upon other
persons. Not only in the matter of personal magnetism,
I mean, but also in the matter of imparting the vibrations of strength and energy. You will notice that other
persons will be conscious of something in your
handshake and touch that will surprise them. They
will not understand just what affects them, but they
will be conscious of some strange feeling pervading
them. The best plan will be for you to keep your secret
to yourself, and to avoid any impression of being out of
the ordinary. You wish to create confidence, not fear —
and the strange and mysterious causes fear rather
than confidence. So keep your own secrets.

CHAPTER 6

GENERATING NERVE-FORCE

By reference to the first paragraph of Chapter IV, you will see that I have separated the physical phase of mental magnetism into two coordinated manifestations, the first of which i.e., the generation within the nervous system of a plenteous supply of nerve-force, I shall now describe.

The word "generation," in this connection, only imperfectly conveys the idea of the actual process of acquiring nerve-force within the nervous system, for the process is one of "absorption" and "distribution," rather than one of "generation." But as the latter term conveys a simpler picture of the process, I have thought well to use it in this connection, particularly as many of the old occult writers have used it, in this sense, before my time.

This process of nerve-force generation may be said to consist of two distinct, yet coordinated phases, viz.: (1) the absorption of an extra amount of nerve-force from the atmosphere, by special forms of breathing; and (2) the distribution of the same to the great centers of the nervous system which act as reservoirs of nerve-force. I shall now proceed to consider these two respective phases, in their proper order.

The first phase of nerve-force generation consists of the absorption of an extra supply of nerve-force from the atmosphere, by means of special forms of breathing. All persons constantly absorb nerve-force from the atmosphere, in the ordinary process of breathing, the amount differing with the individual, or rather, with his habits of breathing. You will have noticed that the vigorous, strong individual, nearly always breathes fully — that is, deeply and regularly — while the weak person will breathe only partially and irregularly. There is a very close connection between full, regular breathing and general physical health and strength, but I shall not touch upon this phase of the subject here, for it forms no part of this special instruction. I merely drop a hint, which the wise will take advantage of.

Without wishing to lead you into the subtleties of Oriental psychology, with its complicated forms of breathing for psychic and spiritual development, etc., I must call your attention, at this point, to the philosophy underlying some of the Oriental breathing practices, for the same is based on the soundest scientific principals. The Oriental philosophy teaches that each mental and physical state of the individual is represented by a special rhythm of breath, the rhythm and condition always being found together. The mental or physical condition will invariably manifest the particular rhythm of breath, which belongs to it; and, likewise (and this is one of the occult secrets) the deliberate assumption of a particular rhythm of breath will speedily result in the manifestation of the appropriate physical or mental condition.

∴

You have but to consider the subject for a moment, to see that when you are frightened or angry, you breathe with a different rhythm than when you are calm and peaceful. Each emotion, up and down the scale, has its own appropriate rhythm of breath, which invariably manifests at the same time. Moreover, different physical conditions like wise manifest in coordinated breath-rhythms. Keep a close watch on yourself, and those around you, and you will soon see that the above statements of facts are strictly correct. You will wonder why you never noticed the phenomena before.

A little less known, even, is the correlated fact that the deliberate assumption or "acting out" of the particular breath–rhythm related to a particular emotion, will result in a speedy experiencing of the emotion itself. This also may be tested out on yourself.

You will find that a few moments' anger-breath or fear-breath (if well acted out, or assumed faithfully) will result in you soon experiencing a feeling of anger or fear, as the case may be. Likewise, you will find that the deliberate assumption, on your part, of the breath-rhythm of peace, calm, self-control, will be sufficient to induce that particular state of feeling in you. There is a big hint in this last sentence, by the way, for that is exactly what the Oriental sages do to induce and maintain the mental state of philosophic calm for which they are noted. In this connection, let us remind you that when you are endeavoring to control your temper, and to maintain your pose, under extreme provocation, you will find that you instinctively strive to control your breath-rhythm, which shows a marked tendency to fly off into a state of rapid panting and gasping. And, so long as you can maintain your steady controlled rhythm of breath, you will maintain your poise and self-control.

Well, to make a long story short — to get right down to the gist of the subject of the absorption of nerve-force through controlled breath-rhythm — let me say to you (1) that there is a breath-rhythm which nature uses to restore nerve-force to the depleted system, after a great demand upon it in the direction of either a strong mental or emotional strain, or after a severe physical strain; and (2) that a deliberate assumption or "acting out" of this particular breath-rhythm will result in your being able to quickly absorb a greatly increased supply of nerve-force for the purpose of use in personal magnetism — to render you full of physical magnetism, in fact. Do you catch this point? If not, re-read the above paragraph, several times, until you fully grasp the importance of the statements therein contained — for they comprise exactly on e-half of the philosophy of nerve-force generation — and much more besides if you are able to grasp it.

You naturally ask, at this point: "What is this particular breath-rhythm which nature uses to aid us in recuperating, and which nature uses to aid using recuperating, and which may be assumed with such wonderful result?" Very well, let me answer you by asking you another question, namely: "How do you breathe when you begin to recuperate just after a severe emotional, mental or physical strain, when the characteristic first panting breath quiets down?" If you will consider carefully, you will answer that you generally begin by one or two long drawn out sighing breaths, followed by a period of calm, deliberate, slow, deep breaths. You may not have noticed it, but these last calm, deep breaths are marked by a slow but regular rhythm — as regular, indeed, as the slow swing of the pendulum of a large clock, or the accompanying "tick" thereof. You will find that this slow, regular rhythmic breath continues for some little time, until you feel refreshed and reinvigorated, when the breath will drop into the normal "everyday" rhythm, and the task is over.

Well, this is exactly the breath-rhythm, which, if properly assumed and well "acted-out," will result in drawing to you a greatly increased supply of nerve-force from the universal storehouse of the same, i.e., the atmosphere around you.

I ask you, student, to pause at his point, and reread the preceding paragraph. Consider it carefully, roll it over in our mind, until you fully grasp its tremendous significance, and fully make it your own thought. For in those few lines is condensed a statement of wonderful truth, which, if taken advantage of, will transform you into a very giant of physical magnetism. Do not proceed with this reading, until you have fully grasped the importance of the information just given you.

But do not imagine that you can jump at once into this great power. You must first gradually acquire the exact rhythm for yourself — for I can do no more than to indicate it to you. I cannot say, "Breathe in just so many seconds; hold the breath just so many; and then breathe out just so many," and so on, as many teachers have done — some who should have known better, for that matter. For each person has his or her own particular breath-rhythm of this kind, the difference arising from mental or physical formation and characteristics.

The following is the rule — the only rule — in this matter: "Ascertain, first, the precise breath-rhythm which nature has given you for use in moments of recuperation after extreme mental, emotional or physical strain; and then, second, practice the same voluntarily by assuming, or acting out the mental and physical conditions producing it, until the rhythm becomes fixed in your memory, so that you can easily reproduce it, instinctively, when you wish." Read this rule over until you thoroughly understand it.

You will find it somewhat difficult to assume or act out the conditions producing the rhythm, at first, unless you happen to be a natural or well-trained actor. But keep trying, until you master it. Practice will make perfect, in this as in everything else, remember. Mentally place yourself in the same vibrations as when you were under some great strain of mind, emotion or body, in the past; and you will find that the same will be followed by an acting-out of the period of recuperation, with its accompaniment of appropriate breath-rhythm. Each student will manage this in his, or her, own way, and will get the result, if persistent, persevering effort were made.

You will find that the first indication of the recuperating breath-rhythm will usually be a long drawn out sigh, followed by a moment of rest, which, in turn, is followed by an easy, though deep, slow, deliberate succession of in-breathing and out-breathing, in perfect rhythm, which will be accompanied by a feeling of increased strength and vitality, of mind and body — delighted to experience is the feeling of "relief" and fresh vigor, vitality and vim which results from this breath-rhythm.

In practicing this recuperative breath-rhythm for the purpose of resting, gaining strength, or increasing your store of nerve-force, do not fall into the too-common error of artificial rhythmic breathing. Do not make the mistake of trying to count the seconds of the breath; or to make the breaths extend neither over a particular time, nor to exactly match each other; or to retain the breath any special time; nor to count time between breaths; or anything of that kind. Forget all about the artificial standards, and give yourself up entirely to a peaceful, calm feeling of relief and recuperation, which nature will bestow upon you if you will create the right conditions for the manifesting of her power. Do not be artificial — trust nature to "run the thing" aright and leave everything in her hands.

Do not bother at this point, to wonder just how many times a day you must practice this exercise in order to gain physical magnetism and absorb nerve-force. That point will be covered in a latter chapter, in connection with the accompanying process of nerve-force distribution — the sole thing before you now is to learn how to produce this breath-rhythm, and to practice until you can produce it at will, easily and naturally, without effort or strain — instinctively, in fact. Until you accomplish this, there is no use of your bothering yourself about the succeeding stages.

And, now a word about practicing this step. Do not overdo the thing — make hast slowly. It is a matter of growth and development with you, and you should not try to rush things too rapidly. Let nature proceed to make the process instinctive, and do not fall into the mistake of pulling up the roots of our plant in order to see whether it has grown overnight. It will grow. Never fear. You will know when you are on the right track, and will be aware of your progress, by reason of your increasing sense of vigor, vitality and vim.

Remember, finally, that the secret of the whole this is that you have discovered how nature recuperates the system in times of extreme necessity; and have then learned how to draw upon this sources of energy at will, thereby increasing the supply far above the ordinary. It is just as if you had discovered a bottle containing the elixir of energy which kind Mother Nature uses to recuperate you in times of need; and then you had learned that you could partake of the elixir, daily, or whenever you felt like it; and were consequently enabled to increase your energy and vitality far above the average. The comparison or figure of speech is not exaggerated — for in this secret you have indeed discovered the elixir of vitality, vigor and vim; that is, if you use it aright.

CHAPTER 7

DISTRIBUTING NERVE-FORCE

In the preceding Chapter I have given you general instructions regarding the first phase of nerve-force by means of certain forms of rhythmic breathing. I now proceed to the general instruction regarding the second phase of nerve-force generation, namely, the distribution of the absorbed nerve-force to the nervous system, and particularly to the great reservoirs of nerve-force.

This process of nerve-force distribution naturally follows directly after that of nerve-force absorption, the two being coordinated phases of one of nature's recuperative processes. Just as is the process of the recuperative breath-rhythm, nature's way of restoring to the system a fresh supply of nerve-force to replace that used in the extra-ordinary mental, emotional or physical strain preceding it, so is the process of nerve-force absorption another (or twin) method of nature to distribute the absorbed nerve-force to all parts of the body, strengthening and invigorating, vitalizing and stimulating, each and every part of the body, and at the same time storing up in the great reservoirs of the nervous system a reserve supply of nerve-force for times of future need.

Again you ask: "What is nature's way of distributing the absorbed nerve-force, as above stated, which also is the way in which you state students of personal magnetism may distribute their absorbed nerve-force or physical magnetism?" As in the case of the previous question, I answer, "Go to nature herself, and discover her method." Let us then do so.

Investigating nature's method of distributing physical magnetism or nerve-force, what do we find nature doing just after the person is exhausted by mental, emotional or physical exertion — that is, in addition to the peculiar breath-rhythm. Answer: We find, accompanying the long deep sigh preceding the breath-rhythm, and also, following the rhythmic breathing, a tendency to "stretch" the muscles of the body. Not only do we notice this phenomenon at such times, but also it is to be observed when we awaken in the morning with a yawn, followed by an instinctive stretching of the muscles. We observe the same thing after we have used up nerve-force in listening, reading, studying, etc. — in fact, in any action, which has required concentrated attention. It is always the yawn, the deep sigh, the measured breath, and, finally, the stretching of the muscles.

Now, do not dismiss this matter with a trifling jest, or an amused smile — for this stretching of the muscles in one of nature's most important offices. It is nature's own favorite way of distributing to all parts of the body the nerve-force being absorbed into the system. It is nature's own way of sending a vitalizing and invigorating current to the places in which it is needed. And, moreover, if we will take it seriously; examine the meaning of its process; and then intelligently apply the same in our work of developing physical magnetism, we will have gained an important secret of nature, and one which we will not be willing to part with, once it is applied and turned to account.

In the first place this "stretching" is something far more than a manifestation of laziness, weariness, or fatigue. It is an instinctive action resulting from nature's recognition of the need of a fresh supply of nerve-force, and her rush to supply the needed energy. Do not mistake and confuse causes and effects in this matter.

You will notice, in cases of complete "stretching," a twofold motion, viz.: (1) An extension; and (2) a tensing or contraction of the muscles, in the direction of drawing in the extended limbs or parts of the body. Now note this, both of these motions are forms of "tensing" or contracting the muscles. The extension movements result from the tension or contracting of the opposite set of muscles. The principal muscles of the body are arranged in opposing sets, one being used to push out, and the other to draw in, the limb or portion of the body. You may always count on the presence of these opposing sets of muscles. When in the process of stretching you first extend, and then draw in the limbs, you rally are tensing both of the opposing sets, in turn. For what purpose? Let us see.

∴

Nature's purpose in tensing the opposing muscles, in the above stated case seems to be that of "squeezing out" something from the muscles. And that is exactly what it is — a squeezing out of something. Of what? Of the old, stale, weakened nerve-force of physical magnetism. Why? — To what end? To the end that the supply of fresh, vital, strong nerve-force or physical magnetism may rush in to take the place thereof.

This is equally true in the case of the brain exhaustion, nerve-exhaustion, or muscle-exhausting — for the brain cells, the nerves themselves, and the muscles are kept vitalized and invigorated by the same form of energy, coming from the same source. Moreover, the fresh supply of nerve-force pouring into the muscles and cells, from the great nerve-force reservoirs of the nervous system, leave the latter more or less depleted, and cause them to call for a fresh adequate supply from the universal source. In short, the stretching process sets into operation the whole machinery of the distribution of the system's supply of nerve-force, and results in the whole nervous mechanism being give a new impetus.

This is the secret of the personal magnetism adept's method of distributing a fresh supply of physical magnetism or nerve-force to all parts of the system, at will — thus rendering himself a veritable dynamo of physical magnetism, if he so desires.

But there is more to this method of the student than mere ordinary "stretching," I assure you. The ordinary stretching is simply an elementary form of nerve-force distribution. I shall call your attention to an extension of, and improvement upon, the elementary method. You have probably heard of that from of calisthenics generally known as "the tensing exercises." Well, in that system you may find the seed of a much more efficient system. The tensing system of calisthenics is taught for the purpose of exercising the muscles — only this and nothing more. It has been found to bring about the greatest results, and to greatly develop the muscles and benefit the general system.

Why? "Oh just exercise," replies the physical bodybuilder. But we know better, for while we realize the benefit obtained from these sensible exercises alone, we also understand how such a rational course of exercise must result in greatly invigorating the entire system, by distributing the nerve-force, and as a consequence bringing about the absorption of a fresh supply to the great reservoir centers of the nervous system, do we not?

We have three decided points of advantage over the "tensing exercise" school, as follows: (1) We precede our tensing exercises by rhythmic breathing exercises, thus bringing to our reservoirs a fresh supply of magnetism or nerve-force; (2) we proceed leisurely and almost "lazily," our idea being that of "stretching" as opposed to the idea of vigorous exercise by tensing, the latter being held by the "tensing exercise" school; and (3) we understand the real reason for the tensing, and hence are able to apply it intelligently, instead of in a hit-or-miss style.

The addition of the rhythmic breath, of course, gives a new and novel impetus to the work of nerve-force distribution; in fact the latter cannot be perfectly performed without the former. This the ordinary tensing exercise practitioner almost entirely misses, except in so far as he becomes fatigued by his vigorous exercise, and is forced to breathe rhythmically, as a consequence, thereby unconsciously obtaining at least some of the benefits of the rhythmic breath. With the ordinary tensing exercise the student, once given our key of the rhythmic breath, is enabled to attain results impossible to him before. He sees a great light, as a consequence.

∴

My students of personal magnetism proceed about the exercises for distribution of nerve-force, or physical magnetism, in an entirely different manner from that of the ordinary practitioner of the tensing exercise systems. The latter work themselves into an exhausted condition, under the belief that their muscles will become better developed by such vigorous exercise. As a consequence, many of them wear out as much as they acquire, of muscular development. My students, instead, pursue anything but a strenuous course of exercising in tensing. Instead of moving vigorously, they proceed slowly, calmly and almost "lazily" in tensing the muscles, in turn extending and then drawing in. They keep before them, all the time; nature's own processes of "stretching," and model their movements entirely upon the same. In this way, as a consequence, there in no exhaustion or using up of nerve-force or tissue to any marked extent, but, on the contrary, there is a constant taking in and distribution of magnetism from the centers to the parts, and consequently a marked increase in vigor, vitality and vim. The difference can be understood perfectly only when one practices my exercises for himself or herself.

Finally, it follows that a much greater effect is obtained by one who practices any form of exercises, understandingly, and with full knowledge of the "why" as well as the "how" of the thing — of the theory as well as the practice. When one knows just what he is about, and just what he wishes and expects to obtain, then he has gained half of the battle. Lacking this knowledge, he wastes energy and effort, and does much that had better be left undone, while leaving undone much that should be done. Verily, "knowledge is power" in this case, as in many others.

∴

It is somewhat amusing, though sad, to see these "tensing exercise" people using themselves up in vigorous exercising, and, at the same time, losing nine-tenths of the benefits gained by those practicing the "lazy" stretching exercises, accompanied by the rhythmic breath, as taught to my students.

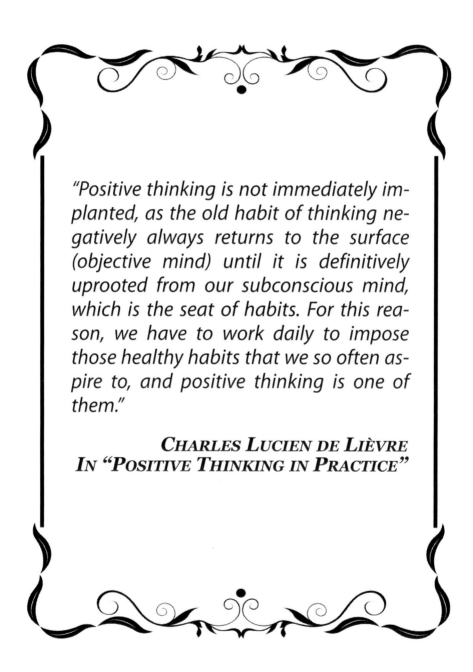

"Positive thinking is not immediately implanted, as the old habit of thinking negatively always returns to the surface (objective mind) until it is definitively uprooted from our subconscious mind, which is the seat of habits. For this reason, we have to work daily to impose those healthy habits that we so often aspire to, and positive thinking is one of them."

CHARLES LUCIEN DE LIÈVRE
IN "POSITIVE THINKING IN PRACTICE"

CHAPTER 8

NERVE-FORCE EXERCISES

I shall now instruct you in the direction of certain forms of exercise designed to generate nerve-force, or physical magnetism, both in the phase of absorption and that of distribution, according to the general principles set forth in the preceding chapters.

ABSORPTION. The exercises, themselves, are designed to give a free and full distribution to the nerve-force or physical magnetism, but the student must always remember that before the nerve-force may be distributed it must first be absorbed. The absorption, of course, is performed by means of the breath-rhythm, according to the instruction already given you.

Important: Remember that every series of distribution exercises must be preceded, and followed, by the practice of the rhythmic breath for a few moments. It will also be found beneficial and useful to interject a short period of rhythmic breathing in between these exercises, from time to time. You will soon discover the need of this, from your own feelings. After you have gained familiarity and ease in practicing the distribution exercises, you will find yourself becoming very sensitive to the inflow of the nerve-force during the breath-rhythm exercise, and in a short time will know by your feelings exactly when you need to absorb more nerve-force during the exercise.

At this point I wish to again remind the student that one of the main features of my nerve-force exercises is that of the entire absence of artificiality, and the presence of "naturalness." I do not give set forms of breathing, to be practiced just so often, for so many minutes at a time. Instead, I give the general principles of the method — the "why" as well as the "how" — and then bid the student to be governed entirely by his own instincts in the matter of the duration of exercises, and frequency of the same.

After a short time the student will fall into the natural habit, just as he does into the habits of eating and drinking, and he will know exactly when he should practice nerve-force generation, and how long he should continue the exercises.

Keep the words "Be Natural" before your mind, and you will make no mistake. Never overdo the exercises, or force yourself to perform them when you do not feel like it. Avoid anything approaching artificiality in the matter. Sometimes you may go a long time without practicing and again you may feel the need of the same very often — in either case follow nature's urgings. Again, you may feel like taking but a moment's exercises at a time — like taking a sip of water, while on other occasions you will feel like taking a long spell of exercise — like taking a deep draught of water when you happen to be very thirsty — follow nature in both instances.

∴

Stretching Exercise. I will begin by calling your attention to a form of exercise which consists of intelligent simple "stretching," but which form of exercise will be found very beneficial. There are a variety of forms of this exercise. I will give you a few general forms, and you may then enlarge on these, and invent combinations, variations, etc.

I. Lying on your back, extend your arms upward over your head, to their full extent — stretch them out easily but thoroughly as far as they will go. Then slowly pull them in. Repeat several times.

II. Stretch the arms sideways from the body — out and then in, several times.

III. Stretch the legs in the same way, several times.

IV. Stretch the neck several times.

V. Stretch the hand and fingers, by moving the hands backward and forward from the wrist, clenching and unclenching the fist: opening and closing the fingers.

VI. Stretch the feet and toes, in the same general manner as in the case of the hands and fingers.

VII. Turn over and lie on your stomach, with the face down on the pillow or floor, and repeat the above exercise in this position. This will bring into play a number of muscles not employed in the former position.

VIII. Rise to your feet and stand with the legs spread out, the feet several feet apart, with arms extended upward and outward. This will bring your body into the general shape of the letter "X." Then rise to your toes and stretch upward as if you were trying to touch the ceiling.

Repeat several times.

You will be surprised at the feeling of rest and renewed strength, which will come to you as the result of the practicing of the above simple stretching exercises. And yet, simple as they are, these exercises perform a great work. You must not lose sight of the fact that when you tense these muscles, in the act of stretching and then contracting the limbs, you really "squeeze out" the old, worn out, depleted magnetism, and absorb in its place a fresh supply of vigor, vitality and vim from the great reservoirs of the nervous system.

Carry in your mind the idea of the sponge, which in order to absorb fully a supply of fresh water, must first be thoroughly squeezed out. The process of the absorption and distribution of nerve-force is very close indeed to the process of the squeezing-out and refilling of the sponge. The following "tensing exercises" are really but an extension of the stretching exercises, more elaborate and complicated, but embodying the same principle. They are useful in energizing the several parts of the body, which are not actively energized by the simple stretching exercises.

SHOULDERS AND CHEST. Stand erect; feet close together; arms at sides. Then draw forward your shoulders, as far front as they will go. Hold the position a moment, and then slowly press the shoulders back as far as they will go. This will tend to energize the shoulders and chest.

The chest may also be energized by taking a few deep, full breaths, which will inflate the lungs and thus extend the chest. The shoulders may also be energized by raising them upward in a "shrug" and then slowly lowering them to original position.

ARMS, WRISTS, AND HANDS. Any simple exercise, which will extend and then contract the arm-muscles, will serve to energize the arms. Twisting them first one-way and then another will do likewise. Twisting the wrist and moving the hands loosely backward and forward from the wrist tends to energize several very important muscles and nerves in this part of the body.

Clenching and unclenching the hands will energize the hands and fingers. Spreading out the fingers fan-shape and then drawing them together will energize the fingers thoroughly.

LEGS, FEET, AND TOES. Follow the general idea of the arm and hand exercises, just mentioned, in the case of the legs, feet and toes. "Squatting" energizes the thighs. Raising up the toes and then lowering to original position energizes the calves of the legs. The "standing-still run" is a good general leg energizer.

NECK. Move the neck forward, as far as it will go, then backward, as far as it will go; then sideways, to the right, as far as it will go – then to the left in the same way; then twist to the right as far as it will go, then to the left in the same manner. These are splendid neck energizers. There are important nerves running through the neck, which are energized by these exercises.

TWISTING AND BENDING. What may be called "a twisting" of the different parts of the body serves to energize the parts very well indeed. In the same way, "bending" exercises are good.

Not only may the legs and arms be twisted easily and effectively, but the entire trunk of the body may be equally effectively twisted by standing erect with feet, say eight or ten inches apart, toes out, and arms hanging easily by the sides; then easily twisting the body to the right, the neck, trunk and thighs being carried as far as they will go; then twisting to the left in the same manner; repeating several times. Bending the body to the right, then to the left, then forward, then backward, is a good energizer.

IN A NUTSHELL. The foregoing exercises might be elaborated into a book by itself — but what's the use? I have given you in a nutshell the main elements of the exercises, and you may do the elaborating yourself. In fact, I can sum up the general principles of the exercises in three words, viz.: STRETCHING, TWISTING, and BENDING. Think over these three words, and you will see that if you will apply them in every possible way to the various parts of the body, you will have a whole system of tensing exercises at your command, without purchasing expensive textbooks on the subject. And, also, remember that in any and all of the so-called "tensing exercises" systems is to be found the best possible principle of nerve-force distribution — always, however, remembering to include the rhythmic breathing according to my previously given instructions. Now, get to work and exercise your ingenuity in devising variations and combinations of the "stretching, twisting and bending" principles. This will energize your mind as well as your body.

ENERGIZING THE SOLAR PLEXUS. The Solar Plexus lies exactly behind the pit of the stomach. It may be energized by practicing a "drawing in" of the abdominal muscles. This may prove a little difficult at first, but a little practice will make perfect. Draw the abdominal muscles "inward and upward" several times at each exercise.

∴

THE SACRAL PLEXUS. The Sacral Plexus is another important plexus, or great center of nerve-force. It is located in front of the lower part of the spinal column — in the region of the hips. It may be energized by a special stretching, bending and twisting of that particular region of the body.

In case of impaired vitality or general weakness, a little extra energizing of these two plexus may be found very advantageous and beneficial, as they directly affect large regions of the body, and important organs.

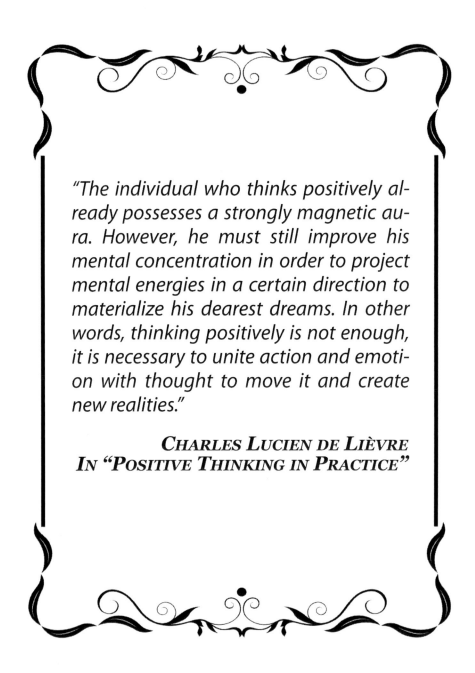

"The individual who thinks positively already possesses a strongly magnetic aura. However, he must still improve his mental concentration in order to project mental energies in a certain direction to materialize his dearest dreams. In other words, thinking positively is not enough, it is necessary to unite action and emotion with thought to move it and create new realities."

CHARLES LUCIEN DE LIÈVRE
IN "POSITIVE THINKING IN PRACTICE"

CHAPTER 9

PROJECTING NERVE-FORCE

At the beginning of Chapter IV, I stated that the physical phase of personal magnetism depends upon two coordinated manifestations of nerve-force, namely: (1) The generation of nerve-force; and (2) the conscious projection, by the will, of that supply of nerve-force into the personal atmosphere, and even to a greater distance under special conditions. I have instructed you regarding the phase of nerve-force generation. Let us now consider the second phase, i.e., that of the projection of the same.

Of all of the mental forces of the individual, the will is the most powerful, and at the same time the one least understood. It is hard even to define the will. Enough for our purpose to realize that it is the power within the mind whereby man is able to do things. Not only does man do the ordinary things of life by means of the will, but also he is able to do some extraordinary things when he learns how.

The old occultist fully realized the mighty power of the will of man; and their teachings convey some very valuable information on this subject. One of their teachings was that by the use of his will man is able not only to project thought-waves from his mentality, but that he is also able to consciously project his physical magnetism, or vital energy, in the same way. The discoveries of the most advanced students of the subject, in our times, verify the old teachings of the occultists in this respect. The system I am herein teaching is therefore based not only on the advanced discoveries of modern science, but also upon the world-old teachings of the ancient occultists. Truth knows no special age or time — it is the property of the ages.

The average man projects his physical magnetism, or nerve-force, into his personal atmosphere, or aura, more or less unconsciously — just as he walks or breathes, for that matter. He has naturally acquired the habit, and does not concern himself about the matter — in fact, he is usually unconscious of and ignorant of the process itself. The differences in the degree of physical magnetism projected or radiated by such persons is determined solely by the degree of nerve-force generated by them, in absence of any special power of projection.

There is a second class, however, the members of which, while not fully informed of their power to project physical magnetism, nevertheless, by their habitual use of the will in the direction of impressing others, powerfully, though unconsciously, direct waves of the nerve-force outward, so that their personal atmosphere becomes well charged with it, and their influence is felt by those coming in contact with it. In this class of individuals will be found the active, energetic, masterful men in various walks of life, who direct others rather than are directed by others, who give orders rather than receive them. These men generally radiate enough physical magnetism to make itself felt by those with whom they come in contact, and are generally felt to be "strong men." But even these persons do not manifest the greatest amount of physical magnetism.

The third class of persons is that composed of individuals who have acquired a greater or less knowledge of fact that physical magnetism may be projected beyond the limits of the brain or body, and who have learned, at least in a degree, the art of so projecting it by the use of the will. These individuals range from those who have acquired merely a glimpse of the truth, up, by degrees, to those who may be spoken of as Masters of the Art. This last named class of persons are those whose power is readily felt and acknowledged, and who leave their impression upon those who come in contact with them.

The projection of the physical magnetism, by the will, is, in a way, a very simple procedure, consisting of two processes, as follows: (1) The belief in, or realization of, one's powers to so project the force; and (2) the actual willing or commanding the force to be projected.

At first it may seem somewhat strange to learn that "belief" has anything to do with this matter, but a little consideration will explain this general law of psychology. It is this way: The will never acts in a direction, which the mind believes impossible. One never tries to reach the moon, because his mind refuses to believe that he can do it — but the child, believing that it is possible, will use his will to move his hand in that direction. The disbelief acts as a brake on the will — do you see the point?

But, you may say, the belief of the child does not enable him to reach the moon. Certainly not, but it caused his will to operate so as to move the hand. Belief does not necessarily render accomplishment certain — but it removes the barriers of disbelief, the latter preventing any accomplishment by the will. There are many things that we would be able to do if we could only believe that we could do — but disbelief acts as a brake and a barrier to the efforts of the will. Realization of one's power will often gain half the battle of accomplishment for him.

In the case before us, the one needs only to believe enough to make the attempt. Then, each time the attempt is made, and one perceives a result, the task becomes easier for the next time. And, at last, the sense of full realization of the power of the will dawns upon the person, and after that the rest is easy.

The second process, i.e., the actual willing, or commanding, by the will, is simply what the words actually say. How can you "will" or "command" the physical magnetism to move into your personal atmosphere, and energize it? — Will it obey me? — you ask. Certainly it will. And the willing or commanding is simply effort the same that you employ, instinctively, when you will or command that your hand be raised. What makes the hand rise? It has no power to raise itself, neither have the muscles any such power in themselves. It is only when you WILL it to move, that things begin to move. The mere willing sends a current of nerve-force over the nerves, and into the muscles, and the hand rises. Sounds simple, doesn't it? And yet it is one of the most wonderful things in the world — only we have grown so accustomed to it that we fail to note the wonder of it all.

The command of the will to the physical magnetism acts in the same manner as the command of the will to the hand. Now, right here, is a point to be remembered. You do not merely say to the hand "raise up." Try it on your own hand — say to it "raise up" without actually willing it to rise, and nothing happens, it is only when you accompany the command with the mysterious effort of the will, that movement occurs.

I cannot tell you how to move your hand by willing — all that I can say is that you must WILL it to rise, and you will understand exactly what I mean. Well, then WILL the physical magnetism to flow out into your personal atmosphere, just as you will the hand to rise, and the thing happens.

But, you may say, you can see the hand move, and know whether your command has been obeyed, while you cannot see the physical magnetism flow. Certainly, but you can feel the magnetism flow, and thus be certain of it.

The flow of physical magnetism soon becomes perfectly apparent to a person, and he is as certain of his radiation as he is that he is radiating heat on a warm day. It is one of those things which cannot well be explained, but which is readily understood by those who experience it.

Try it yourself, and you will soon become conscious of the flow of nerve-force from you, into the field of your personal atmosphere or aura, to a distance of several feet on all sides of you. You will become aware of the effect of your physical magnetism upon others who come in contact with you. You will be able to perceive the reaction and response to your strong magnetic influence on them. They will, unconsciously, let you know that they feel the power of your presence, and acknowledge your strength. You will find a puzzled expression on the part of some of your old acquaintances and associates who will be dimly conscious that there is something different about you, which they cannot explain satisfactorily to themselves. Do not, however, make the mistake of informing them, for this will invite unpleasant comment and criticism, and will also tend to make persons assume a defensive attitude toward you — and even an offensive one, perhaps — in self-protection.

You will also become aware of the healing and strengthening effect of your magnetism upon delicate and sick persons who come in contact with you. Such persons will feel strengthened by your presence, and will dislike leaving you. You may experience some difficulty in preventing them from attaching themselves to you, and seeking to live on your magnetism. But when you learn the art of using the mind-force, or mental magnetism, you will be able to shake them off when necessary. In the meantime, you may do much good by giving these persons magnetic treatments, either by consciously directing a stream of magnetism towards them — by the use of the will — or by the use of the hand. Your magnetism will flow freely out of your hands, and will invigorate weak persons, tend to remove painful conditions, etc. A little experience will make you a "magnetic healer" if you should so desire.

In this matter of hand shaking, you will notice strange things. Persons who take your hand will be impressed by something strange and powerful about you, for your magnetism will flow out toward them and through their body, sometimes in a most marked manner, but more often in an easy current.

You may project your physical magnetism in a direct current, quite a distance from your body, by the simple effort of your will, when once you have learned the little points of practice by repeated trials.

∴

I shall not speak at this place of the use of the physical magnetism in connection with the mental currents, for that topic will be taken up in a later chapter, or chapters rather. But do not wait until that time to practice — get to work and practice with the physical magnetism, now, so that you will have it well in hand when you receive the higher instruction regarding the mental currents. Plant your feet firmly on each step of the ladder — then you will not slip when climbing. Do you see the point?

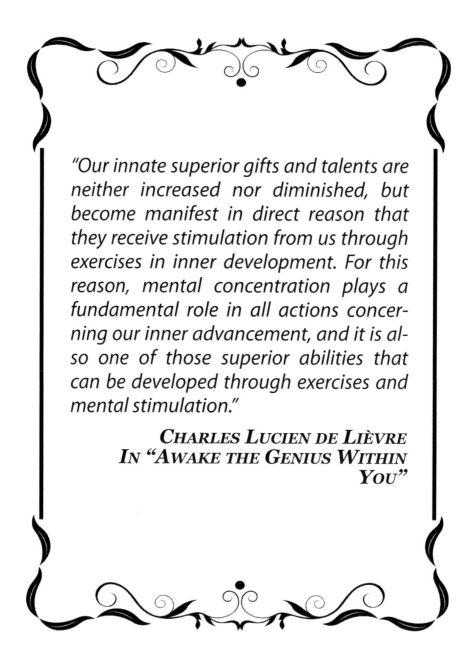

"Our innate superior gifts and talents are neither increased nor diminished, but become manifest in direct reason that they receive stimulation from us through exercises in inner development. For this reason, mental concentration plays a fundamental role in all actions concerning our inner advancement, and it is also one of those superior abilities that can be developed through exercises and mental stimulation."

CHARLES LUCIEN DE LIÈVRE
IN "AWAKE THE GENIUS WITHIN
YOU"

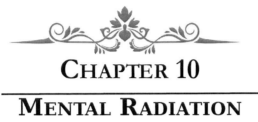

CHAPTER 10

MENTAL RADIATION

L eaving for the moment the phase of physical magnetism, or nerve-force, and entering into a consideration of the other phase, namely, that of mental magnetism or thought-force, let us first take a general glance at the report of the most advanced science of the day, upon the subject of the phenomena of mental radiation.

It will be well for you to feel fully convinced of the reality of this phenomenon, before you undertake to manifest the power. This not only to maintain consistency and mental honesty on your own part, but also that you may rid yourself off of any doubt or unbelief in the matter, the result of such doubt or unbelief being to interpose a barrier or brake upon the will, as we have stated in a preceding chapter.

Listen to the following words from the pen of one of and world's great scientists, Professor Ochorowicz, who has created such a wonderful stir here in Paris by his demonstrations of practical psychology, mental photography, etc. Professor Ochorowicz says: "Every living being is a dynamic focus."

"A dynamic focus tends ever to propagate the motion that is proper to it. Propagated motion becomes transformed according to the medium it traverses. Motion tends always to propagate itself."

"Therefore, when we see work of any kind — mechanical, electrical, nerve, or psychic — disappear without visible effect, then, of two things, one happens, either a transmission or a transformation. Where does the first end, and where does the second begin?"

"In an identical medium there is only transmission. In a different medium there is transmission. You send an electric current through a thick wire. You have the current, but you do not perceive any other force. But cut that thick wire and connect the ends by means of a fine wire; the fine wire will grow hot; there will be a transformation of a part of the current into heat."

"Take a pretty strong current and interpose a wire still more resistant, or a very thin carbon rod, and the carbon will emit light."

"A part of the current, then, is transformed into heat and light. This light acts in every direction around about, first visibly as light, then invisibly as heat and electric current." "Hold a magnet near it. If the magnet is weak and movable, in the form of a magnetic needle, the beam of light will cause it to deviate; if it is strong and immovable, it will in turn cause the beam of light to deviate."

"And all this from a distance, without contact, without special conductors."

"A process that is at once chemical, physical and psychical goes on in a brain. A complex action of this kind is propagated through the gray matter, as waves are propagated in water. Regarded on its physiological side, an idea is only a vibration, a vibration that is propagated, yet which does not pass out of a medium in which it can exist as such. It is propagates as far as other vibrations allow. It is propagated more widely if it assumes the character, which subjectively we call emotive. But it cannot go beyond without being transformed.

Nevertheless, like force in general, it cannot remain in isolation, it escapes in disguise."

"Thought stays at home, as the chemical action of a battery remains in the battery, it is represented by its dynamic correlate, called in the case of the battery a current, and in the case of the brain — I know not what; but whatever its name may be, it is the dynamic correlate of thought. I have chosen the term 'dynamic correlate.' There is something more than that; the universe is neither dead nor void."

"A force that is transmitted meets other forces, and if it is transformed only little by little it usually limits itself to modifying another force at its own cost, though without suffering perceptibly thereby. This is the case particularly with forces that are persistent, concentrated, well seconded by their medium. It is the case with the physiological equilibrium, nerve force, psychic force, ideas, emotions, and tendencies. These modify environing forces, without themselves disappearing. They are imperceptibly transformed, and, if the next man is of a nature exceptionally well adapted to them, they gain in inductive action."

Various other eminent scientists have testified to the general resemblance of the brain to an electrical or magnetic battery or cell group. Professor Bain has said: "The structure of the nervous substances, and the experiments made upon the nerves and nerve centers, establish beyond doubt certain peculiarities as belonging to the force that is exercised by the brain. This force is of a current nature; that is to say, a power generated at one part of the structure is conveyed along an intervening substance and discharged at some other part. The different forms of electricity and magnetism have made us familiar with this kind of action."

Professor Draper tells us that: "I find the cerebrum is absolutely analogous in construction to any other nervous arc. It is composed of centripetal and centrifugal fibers, having also registering ganglia. If in other nervous arcs the structure is merely automatic, and can display no phenomena of itself, but requires the influence of an external agent — the optical apparatus inert save under the influence of light, the auditory save under the impression of sound — the cerebrum, being precisely analogous in its elementary structure, presupposes the existence of some agent to act through it."

Dr. haddock says, in connection with his consideration of the idea that thought may be communicated through ether-vibrations: "The ether is accepted by science as a reality, and as a medium for light, heat electricity, magnetism, etc. The nervous system is certainly comparable to an electric battery with connecting wires. Communication of thought and feeling without the mediation of sense perception as commonly understood is now established.

Inanimate objects exert, now and then, 'strange influences.' People certainly carry with them a personal atmosphere. The representation of the condition of these facts by a psychic field, compared to the magnetic or electric field, becomes, therefore, if not plausible, at least convenient. As such a 'field' exists surrounding the sun, so may a 'field' be assumed as surrounding each human individual. 'We have already strong grounds for believing that we live in a medium which conveys to-and-fro movements to us from the sun, and that these movements are electromagnetic, and that all the transformation of light and heat, and indeed the phenomena of life, are due to the electrical energy which comes to us across the vacuum which exists between us and the sun — a vacuum which is pervaded by the ether, which is a fit medium for the transmission of electromagnetic wares.' By means, then, of a similar theory applied to mind and brain and body, we may find reasonable explanations of many otherwise insoluble mysteries of life, and, which is of more importance, deduce certain suggestions for the practical regulation of life in the greatest individual interest."

Haddock also approvingly quotes the following from Dr. M. P. Hatfield, an authority with whom I, personally, am not familiar: "The arrangement of the nerve-envelopes is so like that of the best constructed electrical cables that we cannot help thinking that both were constructed to conduct something very much alike. I know that there are those who stoutly maintain that nerve-force is not electricity, and it is not, in the sense that an electrical battery is the same things as a live man; but nevertheless nerve-force is closely allied to that wonderful thing that for the want of a better and clearer understanding we agree to call electricity."

Haddock adds: "All states of body and mind involve constant molecular and chemical change. The suggestion arises that the brain, with its millions of cells and its inconceivable changes in substance, may be regarded as a transmitting and receiving battery. The brain being a kind of battery, and the nerves conductors of released stored-energy to different parts of the body, by a kind of action similar to the actions of electricity and magnetism, it is suggested that, either by means of the ether, or of some still finer form of matter, discharges of brain energy may be conducted beyond the limits of the body. If the nerve-track corresponds to wires, this refined medium may correspond to the ether-field supposed to be employed in wireless telegraphy. As electrical movements are conducted without wires, or other visible media, so may brain-discharges be conveyed beyond the mechanism of the battery, without the intervention of nerves — except, as they may constitute a part of the battery. Generally speaking, such discharges would originate in two ways: by direct mental action, or by mental or physical states — perhaps by a combination."

In the above quotations, there will be found constant reference to vibrations in the universal ether. That there is a place, and plenty of room, in the scale of etheric vibrations for the vibrations of mental-force, may be seen by a reference to the following quotations from eminent authorities:

Professor Gray has said: "There is much food for speculation in the thought that there exists sound waves that no human ear can hear, and color waves of light that no eye can see. The long, dark, soundless space between 40,000 and 400,000,000,000,000 vibrations per second, and the infinity of range beyond 700,000,000,000,000 vibrations per second, where light ceases, in the universe of motion, makes it possible to indulge in speculation."

∴

Professor Williams has said: "There is no gradation between the most rapid undulations or trembling that produce our sensation of sound, and the slowest of those which give rise to our sensations of gentlest warmth. There is a huge gap between them, wide enough to include another world of motion, all lying between our world of sound and our word of heat and light. And there is no good reason whatever for supposing that matter is incapable of such intermediate activity, or that such activity may not give rise to intermediate sensations, provided there are organs for taking up and sensifying these movements."

A recent writer in the "London Post" says, "The knowledge we gain by experiment brings home to us what a miserably imperfect piece of mechanism our bodies are. The ear can detect the slow-footed sound vibrations that come to us at the rate of between 40 and 40,000 a second. But the whole of space may be quivering and palpitating with waves at all sorts of varying speeds, and our senses will tell us nothing of them until we get them coming to us at the inconceivable speed of 400,000,000,000,000 a second, when again we respond to them and appreciate them in the form of light."

Another writer, an American psychologist, carries on the tale from this point, as follows: "The first indications of warmth comes when the vibrations reach the rate of 35,000,000,000,000 per second. When the vibrations reach 450,000,000,000,000 the lowest visible light ray manifests. Then comes the orange rays, the golden yellow, the pure yellow, the greenish yellow, the pure green, the greenish blue, the ocean blue, the cyanic blue, the indigo, and finally the violet, the highest degree of light which the human eye can register, and which occurs when the vibrations reach the rate of 750,000,000,000,000 per second. Then come the ultra-violet rays, invisible to human sight, but registered by chemical media. In this ultra-violet region lie the 'X Rays' and the other recently discovered high degree rays; also the actinic rays which, while invisible to the eye, register on the photographic plate, sunburn one's face, blister one's nose, and even cause violent explosions in chemical substances exposed to them, as well as acting on the green leaves of plants, causing the chemical change of transforming carbonic acid and water into sugar and starches. These forms of 'dark light,' that is, light too fine to be perceived by the human eye, are but faint indications of the existence of still higher and finer vibrations — the 'finer forces of nature.'"

Oh, yes! There is plenty of space and room in Nature's scale of forces, for the vibrations of mental energy, nerve-force, and personal magnetism, which combines the two. I trust that the foregoing statements of scientific fact have cleared your mind of any lurking doubts on the subject.

CHAPTER 11

MENTAL ATTITUDES

In a preceding chapter, I have stated that the mental phase of personal magnetism consists of two coordinated manifestations of mental power, the first of which was "the holding of certain mental states until the mental atmosphere becomes charged with the vibrations of the particular mental states." Let us now consider what are these "certain mental states" which are to be held.

In the first place, these "mental states" are not so much any set of particular thoughts, but rather are stated mental attitudes in relation to oneself and the outer world of men. A man's mental attitude, if firmly defined and as firmly held, impresses itself upon everything around the man. His looks grow to conform; his voice; his walk; his general appearance; all grow to reflect his inner states of mind. Moreover, his mental atmosphere becomes so charged with certain vibrations that those who come in contact with the man actually feel his mental attitude, and adjust themselves to it.

Who of us cannot recall the "so meek and humble," Uriah Heep mental attitude manifested by some persons of our acquaintance? Who does not remember having actually felt the sneaky, foxy mental attitude of certain other persons? And who can forget the bold, masterful, mental attitude of certain successful men in our field of business acquaintance? Each of these classes is possessed of a mental atmosphere, which reveals itself at once to us, when we meet them.

I need scarcely urge upon you the importance of producing in yourself the most desirable kind of personal atmosphere. And, as I have said, the mental atmosphere is the direct result of the mental attitude of the person, and reflects the same inevitably. Of course, the mental attitude of a person is composed of a variety of beliefs, opinions, views, ideals, etc., and must of necessity be of a somewhat mixed character. In the case of the majority of persons, the personal atmosphere lacks force and character because of a lack of any particular mental color. But, in the case of the strong individuals of the race, it will be found that there is always a strong fixed mental attitude — a strong desire which colors all the thought; a powerful ambition which gives tone to all the rest; or a firm resolve which fires the entire mental character. This strong vibration is carried out into the personal atmosphere, and its influence is felt, and men react thereto.

In a general way, mental attitudes may be divided into two classes, viz.: (1) positive and (2) negative.

It is difficult, at first, to give the keynote of each of these two classes of mental attitude, but I call your attention to the words of an American writer, in this connection who well says: "That which tends to render one strong, is positive; that which tends to render him weak, is negative." I do not think that I can improve on this definition, and I advise you to adopt it, and to measure your mental attitudes by that standard.

By all means cultivate and develop the positives, and restrict the negatives, in your mental make-up so that, in the end, your mental attitude may be "positive" instead of "negative" — strong instead of weak.

An interesting thing about the cultivation of a mental attitude, is that not only does the improved mental attitude tend to impress itself upon others with whom you come in contact, but that it also tends to impress itself upon your own mentality, so that you gradually become more and more fixed in the mental attitude.

Mental attitude resembles yeast, in the sense that if you insert a single bit of the ferment in your mind, it will begin to work, and grow other cells, until it finally fills your entire mind. It tends to reproduce itself. This is true of both desirable and undesirable mental ideas, but — and remember this well — here is a most hopeful and encouraging fact: a positive idea will tend to kill a negative one, so you see Nature is fighting on your side. The best way to kill and destroy negative mental ideas and attitudes is to plant a good crop of positive in their places, and then encourage the fight — the negatives will go under surely. It is like pouring fresh water into a basin of dirty water — in time the water will become clear; or, again, like flooding a room with sunshine — the darkness will be destroyed.

∴

Let us take a little glance at the principal positives and negatives in the list of mental attitudes:

POSITIVES: courage, masterfulness, activity, initiative, dynamic thought, self-esteem, assertiveness, continuity.

NEGATIVES: fear, slavishness, sluggishness, waiting-for-orders, static thought, self-distrust, retreativeness, fickleness.

This list might be extended much further, but I think that you will have caught the idea by this time. Run over the list of the strong positive qualities of the strong men of your acquaintance and endeavor to reproduce them in you. Run over the list of weak, negative qualities of the weak persons you know — and endeavor to "cut them out" of your mental attitudes.

In this work of building-up of mental attitude, remember this: "This mind grows to resemble that upon which it feeds," and therefore, you should "feed" your mind with the very kind of ideas, which you would like to have your mental attitude reflect. For instance, if you desire a mental attitude of Courage, Determination, Masterfulness, Success, etc., you should read stories in which these points of character are brought out; you should frequent the company of this kind of persons; you should constantly hold in your mind the IDEAL of the things you wish to develop in your mental attitude, and you will find that you will naturally find in the outer world the material things corresponding to them. And, remember this, avoid the opposite and negative books, persons and thoughts, as you would poisonous snakes.

It is astonishing how quickly the mind will respond to the steadfast holding of the POSITIVE IDEAL, and the stimulating environment of POSITIVE things. In a short time, there will be set up an instinctive habit of mind, which will select the positive things from its environment and will also reject the negative things. Train your mind to select the right kind of food for itself, and it will soon acquire the habit and perform the work instinctively without any special supervision on your part. Moreover, there will be developed in your mind that which that gifted American writer, Prentice Mulford, once called "The Attractive Power of Thought," by means of which you will draw to yourself the things, persons, books, etc., which will supply you with the particular kind of mental food best fitted to the IDEAL you are carrying in your mind. I shall not discuss this last wonderful phenomenon, but ask you to remember and apply the fact, nevertheless, for it is one of the great forces of nature.

Finally, I advise you to sit down and make a careful, full, and honest chart of your mental characteristics, positive and negative. Then, place a plus sign before the positives, and minus sign before the negative. Then every day run over your plus list, and fix in your mind the idea that these positives MUST be developed; and the negatives MUST be restarted. The development of the positives will come about by the holding in mind of the ideal of them — thus they will develop and increase, like a self-multiplying cell. The negatives may be restricted by developing their opposites — for; this is the application of the law that positives kill out negatives. Upon these two great fundamental laws of practical psychology, one may build a character at will. I will repeat them once more, so that you will fix them in your mind.

I. Feed your positive qualities by ideas of the same kind, in thoughts, books, persons, environment, etc.

∵

II. Restrict or kill-out your negatives, by developing their positive opposites. And, now, for a wonderful plan of developing a positive mental attitude.

This plan has been successfully practiced my many of my students, some of whom stand high in the list of the world's great men.

It is this:

Build up for your own use, an IDEAL PATTERN of that which you wish to be. Map out exactly the characteristics, which you wish to be yours. Then picture, in your mind's eye, an individual possessed of just these qualities — a complete model, or pattern, of that which you wish to be. Then hold that pattern or model, constantly in your imagination. See it ever; think always about it; view it from the inside and the outside; get fully acquainted with it. And, gradually you will begin to grow like your ideal. The IDEAL will begin to materialize in your own character, and your mental attitude will be that of your model.

Do not pass by this rule, because of its simplicity. It has worked miracles for others — why not for you? If you will persist with this plan, your mental attitude will become positive and fixed, and your personal atmosphere will be charged with the strong, positive vibrations, which will proclaim you as a master.

Let this idea be yours, in studying the following chapters, and remember that in this way you can get the best results from the special instruction, which is to follow this chapter.

CHAPTER 12

THE MENTAL ATMOSPHERE

Following the consideration of the first manifestation of the mental phase of personal magnetism in the preceding chapter, we naturally reach the second manifestation of the same, namely: "The conscious projection of the mental current from the brain centers, by the action of the will of the individual."

This "conscious projection," in turn, may be said to consist of two forms of manifestation, viz.: (1) the projection into the personal atmosphere; and (2) the projection of a direct current, under special circumstances, into the mind of another person, for the purpose of direct influence upon him or her. Let us consider these two forms, in turn, beginning with the first named.

As to the nature of the process whereby one may project his mental currents into his personal atmosphere, I would say that the method is almost precisely identical with that whereby one projects his physical magnetism, or nerve-force, into his personal atmosphere, as fully set forth in Chapter IX.

As in the case of physical magnetism, is found that the average person colors his personal atmosphere by the character of his mental states, or rather by the predominant color of his mental attitude, without any special effort on his part. The degrees of color — not its particular kind, remember, but its degree of force — depends upon the degree of mental activity of the person. The person of inactive thought, ideas or feeling, will have an almost colorless personal atmosphere, while the person of the active mind will display a marked degree of thought-color therein.

We find here, also, the second class of persons, who, while not fully understanding the nature of the power, or the processes of projection, nevertheless manifest a high degree of thought color and power in their personal atmosphere. This strong color and power results from the fact that such persons are usually individuals of a high degree of feeling or idealism — that is to say, they experience strong feelings, on the one hand; or else have strong mental ideas of anything in which they are interested — or perhaps both strong feeling and strong idealism.

The strongest color and power manifested by persons of this class, is found in persons who take a strong interest in things. This strong interest really combines the two elements of feeling and attention, respectively. Feeling is a strong mental element; and attention, you will remember, is a direct application of the will. So, it follows, that such persons must strongly project their mental states into their personal .atmosphere, although unconscious of the same, and without a deliberate employment of the will for this purpose.

∴

But, here, as in the case of the physical magnetism, the strongest and most powerful effect is produced by the individuals who understands the process, and who consciously and deliberately project their thought into their personal atmosphere, where it joins and is vitalized by their physical magnetism, so that its full effect is manifested upon those who may come within its field of influence.

The process of using the will in the direction of projecting thought-color and power into the personal atmosphere is practically identical with the use of the will in the case of physical magnetism, or nerve-force, as described in Chapter IX. In other words, it consists of two phases, viz.: (1) belief in one's power to so project; and (2) the actual projection by the will. I have informed you fully regarding the part played by "belief" in this process of projection, and shall say nothing more on this subject here. The use of the will in the matter of projection, here also, consists of the actual willing or commanding of the thing itself.

The mental currents are very obedient to the will, and in fact, depend almost entirely upon the will for power to move and act. And, do not forget this, for it is important, the will is moved largely by desire. If you will strongly desire that your personal atmosphere be colored by your thought currents, and will at the same time picture the thought currents flowing out and filling your personal atmosphere, you will have little left to do in the direction of the conscious use of the will. This because, in the first place, the will naturally operates along the lines of stung desire; and second, because the forming of the mental picture will result in the use of the attention, and the attention, as I have said, is a positive and direct action of the will in the direction of focusing its power. So, you see, by following this plan, you are really setting into operation the power of the will itself, although not by direct command. You may also use the direct command to the will to project the thought currents, just as you use the same to lift your arm or close your eyes.

There is one other important point, though, which you must make note of and actively employ in your work of building up and maintaining a strong positive personal atmosphere. I allude to the process of intermingling and combining the two elements of personal magnetism, i.e., (1) the physical magnetism, and (2) the mental magnetism. While there is a natural combination and intermingling of these two, without any special effort on your part, nevertheless, an enormously greater effect will be obtained by a distinct mental process on your part, in which process is combined the several uses of the will above referred to. This special process consists of three distinct mental operations, as follows:

(1) You must earnestly desire the combination of the two elements of personal magnetism, the physical and the mental forces. You must create the strongest kind of desire for this combination. This desire must be stronger than a mere "want" — it must be fanned up to the stage of an actual "longing" or "craving" for the combination in question. (2) You must use the imagination, actively, in the direction of forming a mental picture of the mingling of the two forms of magnetism, just as you would picture the combination of two clouds, or two currents of water in a lake, flowing in from two different sources. The stronger and more vivid you can make this picture, the stronger and more effective will be the result. I have explained that these mental pictures require the use of the attention, and that the attention is due to a direct and concen-

trated use of the will. Therefore, the will is actively and powerfully employed in this process and the result is correspondingly effective. (3) The direct command of the will itself, in the direction of "willing" the currents to coalesce and combine. These three phases of the use of the will, combined, will prove very effective in the direction names. A little practice will enable you to perform all three of them, at one time, almost automatically.

You will see, by a little thought, that the process just described, is practically that used when you perform any conscious, voluntary motion of the body. Let us see: You wish to raise your hand. What processes are involved? Three, as follows (1) Desire — you wish to raise your hand; (2) mental picture — for almost unconsciously you form the image of the raised hand; and (3) the direct command of the will, which is the final mental effort.

The combination of the two forms of personal magnetism, the physical and the mental, works along two lines of action namely, (1) the mental magnetism gives color and character to the physical magnetism; and (2) the physical magnetism gives vitality and acting force to the mental magnetism. It might be said, almost, that the physical magnetism gives the body and moving force to the combination, while the mental magnetism gives the "soul" to it. Each redoubles the efficiency of the other, by the power of combination.

∴

The occultists inform us that the personal atmosphere is composed of certain colors, depending upon the particular quality of mental states that happen to be predominant in the combination — each mental state being said to have its own color. I shall not take up this phase of the subject, but merely mention it because of its general interest in this connection.

The occultists also inform us that, when the combination of the two elements of magnetism combine, the mental magnetism takes on a deeper and more pronounced color and hue, and appears also to solidify and become denser; and that the physical magnetism seems to be rendered doubly active, its increased energy being evidenced by tiny sparks and dancing glittering atoms. It seems to be like the combination of two different chemicals, each tending to increase the potency and activity of the other, and the two combining in the production of particularly potent and active new thing.

From the same sources, we learn that the aura or personal atmosphere of the person who uses the will in the direction of forming the potent combination of the two forms of magnetism, seems to be almost alive, so filled with energy is it. It is said that when it comes in contact with other persons — particularly when the owner is using his mind to impress and influence the others — the aura will reach out and actually enfold the other persons within its field of energy, seemingly trying to embrace the person and hold his subject to the vibration of its owner's mind.

When you learn to produce this combination effectively, you will begin to notice that you will almost unconsciously affect and influence other persons with whom you come in contact. You will notice that they will begin to take on your moods and general feelings, and that they will fall "in tune" with your mental vibrations, generally. If you are enthusiastic about anything, they will begin to manifest enthusiasm. And so on, each of your mental states registering an effect upon the other persons. Moral: Hold only those mental states, which you wish other to "take on."

And, keep your inner opinions and designs well to the back of your mind, by an effort of the will, and show only what you wish to be sensed by others, for remember your thought currents will have become wonderfully dynamic and powerful.

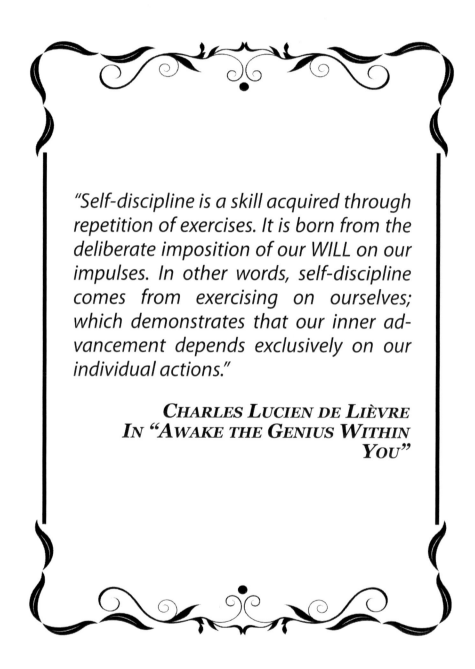

"Self-discipline is a skill acquired through repetition of exercises. It is born from the deliberate imposition of our WILL on our impulses. In other words, self-discipline comes from exercising on ourselves; which demonstrates that our inner advancement depends exclusively on our individual actions."

CHARLES LUCIEN DE LIÈVRE
IN "AWAKE THE GENIUS WITHIN
YOU"

CHAPTER 13
MAGNETIC CURRENTS

The magnetic energy of the person, formed by a combination of his physical and mental force, like all other forms of magnetic or electric force, tends to run in currents, and to be transmitted in waves. The personal atmosphere of the person is, in fact, composed of many waves of magnetic energy, circling around the confines of his aura, a constant wave-like motion being maintained, and a rapid rate of vibration always being manifested.

It is these waves of magnetic energy which, when coming in contact with the mind of other persons, set up a corresponding rate of vibration there, and thus produce a mental state in them corresponding to that of the person sending forth the magnetism. As I have already stated several times, the physical magnetism gives the "body" and energizing quality to this personal magnetism, while the mental magnetism supplies the quality of color or character to it.

At this point I wish to digress for a few moments in order to make clear to your mind the important fact that in charging the mental atmosphere with the combined mental and physical magnetism, it is not necessary to make two distinct and separated efforts of the will. In describing and explaining to you the process of sending for the currents of physical magnetism, and mental magnetism, respectively, I have been compelled to take up each phase separately, and describe the action of the will in the process of projecting each of these phases of personal magnetism. And, if I were to say no more on this point, the student might be left with the impression that in order to fully charge his personal atmosphere with the combined waves of physical and mental magnetism, he would have to first charge it with one kind of magnetism, and then with the other. This is not correct, for a combined effort of the will is all that is required, as you shall now see.

It is possible to combine the mental picture of the two forms of personal magnetism, the physical and the mental, into one image or idea in the mind. It is also possible to combine the two into the desire or inclination to project the energy. And, it is equally possible to combine the projection of the two into one effort of the will. It is a simple thing — as simple as that of twisting two silk threads; threading them into the eye of a coarse needle; and then taking stitches with the needle. Think of the physical and mental magnetism as two twisted threads inserted into the eye of your needle of will, and then think of your passing these threads together into the fabric, by simply pushing the needle through. This illustration will enable you to form a clearer mental picture of the process.

You will find that after a little practice you will instinctively combine the two threads in the eye of the needle of your will. At first you may find it easier to first think of the physical magnetism, and then of the mental — so to speak, threading first the one thread and then the other. But after very little practice you will find it easier to take up the two threads at once, giving them a little twist together, and then passing both of them through the eye of the will-needle at the same time. Remember, then, learn to "twist together" the threads of the two kinds of magnetism, so that the will may push them both through at the same time.

You should keep the personal atmosphere well charged at all times, by projecting magnetism into it several times a day. No special times or number of times is absolutely necessary — you must use your own judgment and feeling in this matter. You will soon learn to feel when your magnetic aura is weak, and when it is strong. These things come to one by practice and actual experience, and cannot very well be taught except through actual experience. You will soon learn what it is to "feel" the condition of your magnetism, just as you now feel heat or humidity, or the reverse thereof.

If you are about to come into contact with others whom you wish to influence; or, on the other hand, if you are about to come in contact with others who may want to influence you; you should charge yourself well with magnetism — that is to say, you should generate and project into your personal atmosphere a large amount of magnetism, which will thus render your aura strong and positive, instead of weak and negative. The principal thing in battle is to be fully prepared for any emergency, and this rule is applicable to the case of the uses of personal magnetism in your dealing with other persons.

∴

Remember, then, to combine the idea and image of the combined magnetism when projecting or charging with personal magnetism — the two twisted threads in the needle, remember.

Now, to return to the subject of magnetic currents:

The currents of magnetism not only constantly flow around within the limits of the aura, but also often push forward toward other persons who attract the attention of the person. In such cases, the aura seems to stretch out toward the other persons, and even to envelop them in its folds. Remember, I am now speaking of the involuntary action of the aura or magnetic currents, not of the conscious and deliberate projection of the currents from the mind to the other mind. There is an almost automatic action of the aura or magnetic currents in the way just stated, when another person arouses the interest or attention of the person.

Of course, if you insist upon the strictest scientific interpretation of this apparently automatic movement of the currents, I must admit that even in such cases the will of the person is the direct cause of the projection. For, it must be remembered, that in the mental acts of interest and attention there is a non-deliberate action of the will — an automatic action, so to speak. The will is called into operation the moment the attention is attracted — in fact; the attention is a positive act of the will. And, consequently, the will sets into motion the magnetic currents in the direction of the object of attention.

So, you will see, when you are conversing with another person, or addressing a number of persons, you are really sending in their direction a series of currents of personal magnetism, the vibrations of which must affect them unless their own vibrations are of a more positive nature. In fact, very many men of the greatest personal force, whose personal magnetism may actually be felt, employ the force in this manner, and make but little use of the "direct flash" methods of immediate concentrated magnetic force, which you will be asked to consider in the succeeding chapters. Their general store of personal magnetism is so great — their personal atmosphere so charged — that mere contact with it produces the result.

But while the above general method of magnetic influence is very effective, provided the individual has learned to sufficiently charge himself, it still remains that the method is that of the shotgun, as compared to that of the rifle, and uses up much power while a smaller amount would suffice. Everything points to the value of a concentrated force, rather than that of the scattered energy. At the last, however, the best method is that which employs both the shotgun and rifle methods — the rifle bullet going right to the mark, surrounded by a cloud of flying shots which completes the work, and renders success certain. So, therefore, when you become interested in the "direct flash" methods in the succeeding chapters, do not lose sight of the important part in personal influence played by the general effect of the magnetism of the aura.

Before I leave this subject, I wish to explain a certain bit of phenomena, which has puzzled many students of personal magnetism. I allude to the apparently unconscious use of magnetic power, which we so often witness. For instance, you may be thinking intently of some other person, without any conscious intention of influencing them in any manner, and yet, when you meet the person afterward, or hear from him, you will find that your magnetic currents have influenced him, often very markedly so. This is puzzling, when you remember that you made no effort to influence the person by the "direct flash" method, and when you remember that the person was far removed from your personal atmosphere or aura. What is the answer you ask?

The explanation is this: By your concentrated attention and interest, you have actively (though unconsciously set the will into motion, and the result is that there has been projected toward the other person a current of your magnetism — a great stretching out of your personal atmosphere in his direction — and he has been affected by it just as if he had been in your presence. Of course, the other person will not be greatly affected by your currents, unless these happen to be charged with great physical magnetism, and strongly colored by your mental status. But, nevertheless, there will always be some influence exerted, unless, indeed, the other person is more positive, magnetically, that are you, in which case he will not be affected in the least.

So you see, we not only are constantly surrounded by an aura or atmosphere of our magnetic currents, but are also more or less unconsciously sending forth currents of our magnetism into the aura of others, which exert more or less influence upon them. In the same way, the currents of others are constantly reaching our aura, and exerting more or less influence upon us, unless we happen to be more positive than they, in the matter of our vibrations — or (note this), unless we deliberately use an effort of the will in the direction "shutting the door" on these outside vibrations.

CHAPTER 14

THE DIRECT FLASH

We now approach a phase of the general subject of personal magnetism, which is highly important, as well as most interesting to the student, because of its striking and startling features. This phase consists of the deliberate, conscious projection of personal magnetism into the aura of another person, or persons; or into the atmosphere of a crowd of persons. This method has been called the "direct flash," because it resembles the flash of the electric spark, rather than the diffused discharge of a steady current of electricity.

The "direct flash" is the method employed in projecting a positive influence in the direction of others — a mental command backed up by the combined physical and mental magnetism. The method is: (1) The forming in the mind of a direct command accompanied by a mental picture of the desired action on the part of the other person; (2) the mental gathering of the two combined forms of magnetism into one force; and (3) the deliberate discharge of the "flash" by the will.

You have been fully instructed regarding the first two phases of this "direct flash" method; and you have been given general information which will enable you to comprehend the third phase, i.e., that of the "deliberate discharge of the 'flash' by the will." That is to say, you understand the forming of the mental picture, and the projection of magnetism, in connection with the gathering up of the two forms of magnetism; and you likewise are acquainted with the power and action of the will in the work of projecting magnetism. All you need to complete the instruction regarding the method of using the "direct flash" is a little further instruction regarding the use of the will in projecting this "deliberate discharge." And this further instruction I shall now give you.

The key to the "direct flash" consists in the deliberate action of the will in projecting or "flashing" into the mind of the other person a certain direct statement or command, backed up by all the magnetic forces within you. This comes easily and rapidly as the result of a little practice. And, moreover, you may practice in private, standing before your mirror, until you acquire the mental mechanical ease, which is necessary.

Let us now begin with some concrete examples, rather than continuing the general consideration. In other words, let us now "get down to brass tacks," in the matter.

Preliminary Exercise. Stand before your mirror; gaze positively and firmly at your own image therein, just as you would gaze toward another person. In fact, you must try to imagine that you are really gazing at another person. Then, send that imaginary person — pictured by your reflected image — the message: "I am stronger than you!"

Now, try to get my exact meaning, as I proceed. You must not rest content with merely thinking or saying the words of the magnetic command above given — you must cultivate and develop an actual willing the command, just as you would will the raising of your hand, or the clenching of your fist. You will find it necessary to cultivate this power of so willing, for your belief will not at first coordinate with the will. You could not very well will your hand to be lifted, or fist clenched, unless you actually believed that the thing itself were possible. In the same way the little child has to first learn the possibility of using his will, deliberately, in performing physical actions. He first sees others performing certain actions, and the idea gradually dawns upon him that he, too, may do them. Then he begins to use his will, awkwardly at first, in directing the muscles as required. In the same way will you have to develop your ability to use your will deliberately in the direction of this form of personal magnetism? But by a little steady, earnest practice before the mirror, you will soon master the mechanism of the thing — the rest will be all a matter of practice upon persons.

In sending the message, "I am stronger than you," you must accompany the effort of the will (by which you send forth the thought-command) with a strong mental conviction that your are stronger (magnetically) than him, and also with the belief that he will be impressed by this fact and will accept your statement. You must get yourself into the mental attitude of demanding that he accept your statement, not that you merely request him to do so. In this form of magnetic influence there is no such thing as "requesting" — it is all a matter of "insistent command" — do not forget this. When you merely request, you usually take second magnetic position, giving to the other person the first place. But when you command, you take the first place, yourself, and push him into the second. In practicing before your mirror, remember this, and endeavor to raise yourself into the first position. You will know when you have done this, by the peculiar feeling of superior magnetic strength that you will experience.

After having mastered the above exercise to your own satisfaction — that is, until you have thoroughly acquired the feeling of mastery, and magnetic superiority, when you send forth the flash of command — you may proceed to the following, which is based upon the first, and results from it. I mean, that you are now in a position to practice this second stage of the exercise before the mirror. You will feel like beginning to try your power upon other persons, but you would do better to wait until you have thoroughly mastered the mechanism of magnetism before the mirror.

This second stage of the preliminary mirror exercise is summed up in the word of mental magnetic command, which you address to the imaginary person represented by your reflected image, viz.: "I can command you to act." This, as you will see by a careful consideration of the words, is really a tremendously powerful statement, and it will require a great exercise of our power of belief, and mental imagery, to get yourself into the proper mental state, so that the will may travel easily on its path to enforce the command. Remember, that in order for the will to be able to move smoothly over its channel, so that it may reach the mark, it is necessary that you clear away any obstacles that may remain in your own mind. It is enough for the will to have to fight and break down the obstacles in the mind of the other person, without also being called on to combat and overcome the obstacles in our own mind. So, you must get yourself in the proper mental state, before you can hope to influence others.

When you send forth the mental command to the reflected image, you must concentrate a tremendous power of meaning in the statement, "I can command you to act." The statement must be accompanied by the full force of your own conviction and belief that you can so command, and that you will be obeyed. And, in order to do this, you will have to arouse in yourself the full consciousness of your own magnetic force, so that you can fairly feel it vibrating in and around you. You will have to re-read these instructions several times before they will become perfectly clear to you. In fact, you will have to begin practicing, and then re-reading them between exercises, before you will get the full meaning. The meaning will gradually unfold into your understanding, as you proceed with your practicing. It is just as if I were giving you directions as to mastering the art of skating — you would not really grasp the full meaning of the instructions until you began actually practicing on the ice — and each time you would refer to the book, you would perceive a new meaning to the words. So it is in the case before us — you will understand the instructions fully only when you begin the actual practice.

Now, after you have gotten to the point in the mirror-practice where you are able to actually feel that you have sent forth to the reflected image the command that you are stronger, thereby forcing the other person into the second magnetic place — and also that you can command the other person to act as you will, thereby placing him in the subordinate capacity of action — you may proceed to try upon the reflected image some special commands in the same spirit. Now do not fall into the error of supposing that all this mirror-practice is merely "child's play." If you do, you will be making a great mistake, for it is anything but play or idle pastime. It is the learning of the mechanism of the "direct flash," before you start in to run the machine in earnest. It is like the period of preliminary practice in anything, which precedes the actual performance. It is the rehearsal, which must precede the play. Do not fail to faithfully perform the rehearsal exercises, before you begin to manifest your magnetism in earnest. You must fully acquaint yourself with your magnetic machine before you begin to run it in earnest.

The preceding practice exercises may be followed by a similar practice of sending forth "flashes" of anything that you may wish to actually send to other persons later on. You may supply these commands for yourself, or you may practice on the following excellent commands, all of which are likely to be used by you in your actual manifestation of personal magnetism.

These commands may be varied, of course, to suit your tastes. They must all be delivered before the mirror, in exactly the same manner as I have already stated:

"Look at me!"

"Give me your full attention!"

"Come this way!"

"Go away from me — let me alone!"

"You like me." "You love me"

"You feel like doing as I wish you to do!"

"You want to please me!"

"You will agree to my proposition!"

"Get out of my way!"

"You are attracted toward me!"

"I fascinate you!"

"I am your MASTER!"

"Come! Be quick, and do as I tell you!"

"You are receptive to my wishes!"

"You are responsive to my will!"

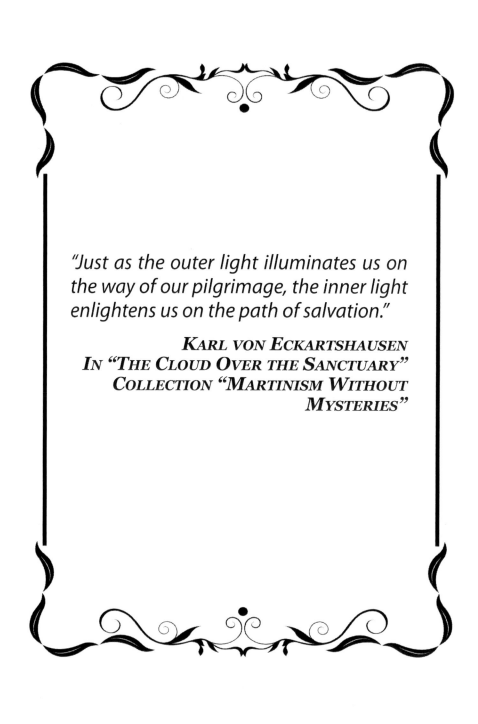

"Just as the outer light illuminates us on the way of our pilgrimage, the inner light enlightens us on the path of salvation."

KARL VON ECKARTSHAUSEN
IN "THE CLOUD OVER THE SANCTUARY"
COLLECTION "MARTINISM WITHOUT
MYSTERIES"

CHAPTER 15

EXERCISE IN THE DIRECT FLASH

And, now, having mastered the preliminary mirror-exercises, you are ready to begin your experiments on real persons. But, here, too, you must crawl before you can walk and run. You must begin with the simpler forms of magnetic influence, before you can accomplish the more complicated or difficult tasks. But, you have now emerged from the kindergarten stage, and are ready to practice in earnest. If you have faithfully followed the instructions in the mirror-practice, you have mastered the mechanism of magnetic influence, and are ready to "run the machine" in pubic view. But do not for a moment lose what you have gained in the mirror-exercise. Hold tight and fast to the "technique" you have acquired, and do not for a moment fall into the error that you must now begin all over again. The thing for you to remember, always, is that you are really but carrying the mirror-exercises forward on a higher scale, in a broader field. And you will find some interesting work ahead of you. Take my word for it.

∴

First Exercise. I shall now give you an exercise that is almost always given to beginners by the best teachers of magnetism. It consists of the process of causing a person ahead of you, on the street, to turn around as if he had heard some one call out to him by name. The process is very simple. You have but to walk some little distance behind the other person, on the street, park or other public place. Concentrate your fixed attention on the person, gazing at the lower back part of his head. And sending him first a strong flash of magnetic force, this being followed by the "direct flash" command; "Here you! Turn around," just as if you were actually calling out aloud to him. You may even whisper the words so softly that no one else can hear them — this may help you to put force into the command at first, but you will soon outgrow the need of the same. At the time you send the flash command you must actually WILL that the person will around in your direction. Put all the magnetic force within you, in this effort.

You will find that in some cases the other person will turn his head almost at once, and look inquiringly behind him in your direction. In the majority of cases, however, he will take a longer time about it. He will be apt to first grow uneasy and restless, and begin by glancing from side to side, as if looking for some one; then he will almost (but not quite) turn his head around; then, finally he will glance backward somewhat furtively and suspiciously. No two persons act precisely alike in this respect; and, then, again, the same person will act differently under different conditions. There are certain times at which the conditions seem to be more favorable than at others, for various reasons, as you will discover for yourself.

∴

You will find, in this as well as the following other exercises that the best results will be obtained while the other person is proceeding idly along, without his attention being directed particularly in any direction.

When the attention is free, the mind is more open to outside influences. When the other person's attention is firmly fixed on anything else, it will be found difficult to influence him to any marked degree. This is the result of an established rule of psychology, and will be found to be operative in all cases, as for instance, if you call a person when he is preoccupied either with deep thought, or else when his surroundings-he will probably not hear you call him, though under other conditions he would turn readily. The same rule is, of course, operative in the case of magnetic influence.

Second Exercise. When in church, theater or other public place, or even in a room full of company, fix your gaze at the lower back of the head of some person in the place, and send him the "direct flash" command: "Here, you! Turn around and look at me!" Using all the magnetic force within you, and putting the force of your will back of the command.

You will notice the same peculiar result as in the preceding exercise, i.e., the fidgeting in the seat, the uneasiness and restlessness, the final quick turn of the head in your direction, followed by the confused expression of countenance. In both of these cases, you should maintain a calm, uninterested gaze ahead, apparently not noticing the person. It is not well to have persons get the idea that you are experimenting upon them, at any time. There is no power so potent as the silent, reserved power. So keep your own counsel, and do not scatter and weaken your force by talking about it to others — far less by boasting about it. There are certain good psychological and occult reasons for my admonition regarding keeping your own counsel, and not dissipating your energy by talking about it, or revealing it to others. I shall not say more on the subject at this time — but I want you to remember what I have said, and to heed it.

Third Exercise. This is a variation of the first exercise, and consists of making the person ahead of you turn to the right or to the left while walking ahead of you. This may follow your exercise of making him turn around. When he approaches another person, send him a flash to move to the right, or to the left, as you will. You may also command a person in like manner when he is approaching you. You will be surprised at your success in this direction, after a little practice. In the case of a very sensitive subject, you can cause him, or her, to zigzag in a comical manner. Do not overdo this, however, or you may defeat your own object, besides being unkind to the sensitive person.

Fourth Exercise. This is a variation of the second exercise, and consists in making the seated person, in front of you, turn and glance to the right, and then to the left, as you will. During the exercise, which may extend over some time, you may obtain some very marked results from the experiment, in some cases. As before, I caution you against going too far with the experiment, lest you be noticed by others, and also, because it is not fair to the subject.

Fifth Exercise. In this experiment, you command the other person to drop his cane, or umbrella, etc., or her fan, handkerchief, etc. In short, you cause the other person to perform some little muscular action under the control of your will.

Sixth Exercise. The above exercise may be varied by sending passing persons various commands while you are seated at your window, or on your porch, etc. You may put in an interesting hour in sending flashes to the passing crowd, one at a time, of course, and then noting the percentage of successes. You will find that the percentage will vary; but the general degree of success should slowly but steadily increase, on the average. Do not make the tests too complicated, but send the flash to perform some very simple motion. You will be surprised to discover what a large percent of the persons will glance in your direction, even though you have not particularly commanded them to do so. This latter result occurs because of the general attraction that they will feel toward you, by reason of the influence of your magnetic wave.

Seventh Exercise. While I have advised you to look directly at the other persons, in sending the flash, this is not absolutely necessary after you have fully acquired the "mechanism" of the flash. In fact, after a short time, you will be able to obtain the result even though your eyes are turned in another direction. It is not your eye that influences them, but merely that by gazing intently you manage to firmly concentrate your attention and will in their direction. You may try the experiment of gazing straight ahead of you in a public place, or on the street, and then flashing the command to the other person to look at you, and you will find that you will meet with quite a large percentage of success, particularly after you have succeeded with the gazing plan of procedure.

Eighth Exercise. After having mastered the above exercise, you may proceed to a still higher form of magnetic influence, namely, that of influencing the speech of another person. You proceed in this case in the same general manner as in the exercises just given. When a person is speaking to you, you may "put words into his mouth" by a strong mental command, or magnetic flash. Do not try to make him say a whole sentence — at least at first. Rather begin by waiting until he pauses in his speech, and then strongly will a certain word to him — a word that will naturally fit into his sentence — and he will be very apt to repeat it. After a little practice you can make him repeat an absurd word, or to stammer, halt and stutter in his speech, if you so will it. After still more practice, you may succeed in causing him to repeat a whole sentence, or even more, to express the thought you have put into his mind; or to ask some question which you have willed that he should ask.

You will readily see by this time, that a constant practice along these lines, will result in your acquiring the power to will and magnetically influence another person to do many things, in response to your will, and silent command. In fact, a constant development along these lines will make of one a very giant in magnetic power, whose results are proportioned only by the degree of magnetic force of other persons, or the degree of persistent practice and development on his own part.

But I wish to caution you, at this point, against using this power for any unworthy purpose. This caution does not arise from merely a moral motive on my part, but from knowledge of certain psychic laws which cause a "reaction equaling the action," and which will bring sorry results to you if you violate the rule. So long as you use your newfound power for purely scientific experiments, or legitimate purposes of human association, all very well and good. But never prostitute your power to accomplish unworthy or criminal ends, lest you become involved in a storm of your own raising — or enmeshed in a web of our own weaving. There are certain psychical laws, as well as physical laws, which must not be broken — and this is one of them. This is particularly true of the case of a person using the power for the purpose of influencing the other sex in an immoral direction. All the old occult writers' caution particularly against this practice. So heed the advice, and do the right thing only, with your power.

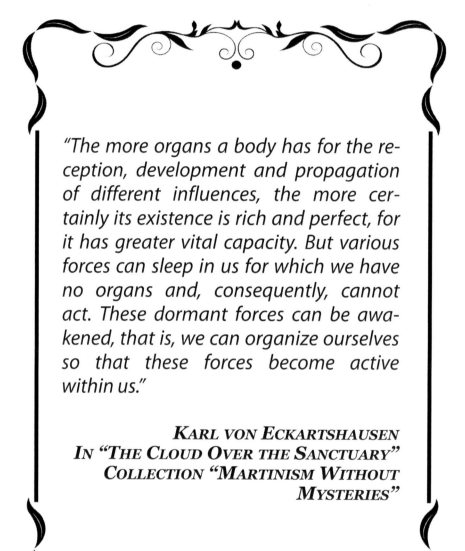

"The more organs a body has for the reception, development and propagation of different influences, the more certainly its existence is rich and perfect, for it has greater vital capacity. But various forces can sleep in us for which we have no organs and, consequently, cannot act. These dormant forces can be awakened, that is, we can organize ourselves so that these forces become active within us."

KARL VON ECKARTSHAUSEN
IN "THE CLOUD OVER THE SANCTUARY"
COLLECTION "MARTINISM WITHOUT
MYSTERIES"

CHAPTER 16

THE POSITIVE AURA

Now that you have mastered the technique of the mechanism of the "direct flash," you are ready to proceed to the actual demonstration and contact with the general public. But, before taking up that phase of the subject, I think it well to ask you to consider the matter of the creation and maintenance of the positive aura. I have purposely postponed the consideration of this phase of the subject, until we reached this particular point in the instruction, because, in order to properly create and maintain the positive aura, it is necessary that one understands the mechanism and technique of the "direct flash," for he will need to manifest the same power in the case of the positive aura. But, now that you have mastered the technique or mechanism of the "direct flash," you are ready to receive the instruction regarding the positive aura, and we may as well proceed to consider it at this very point.

I have already given you instructions regarding the cultivation of a desirable personal atmosphere, or aura, and need not repeat here what I have already said elsewhere. But, a moment's consideration will show you that there will arise certain conditions or occasions in which you will find it very desirable to be able to influence a number of persons en masse — the crowd as a whole — rather than to send the "direct flash" to each of the individuals separately. Of course, the crowd will be influenced by your general personal atmosphere, but you now need something more positive, and more to the point. And the "positive aura" is what you must acquire to satisfy this requirement.

The positive aura is simply the general personal atmosphere, but directly and positively charged by a concentrated effort of the will — the same effort, in fact, as that made in the case of the "direct flash."

Let me illustrate the "positive aura" by means of several stories from real life — the experiences of several students of mine. These personal experiences will give you a better idea of just what is needed than would pages of general instruction on the subject. The little stories are not fiction, remember, but are "taken from life," and are bits of human documents from the lives of real people, all of which have come under my personal observation and consideration.

Several years ago, in Paris, I had a student whose real strength of character was marred by her abnormal self-consciousness, shyness, timidity, and sensitiveness — in fact; in the word "sensitiveness" you have the keynote of this young woman's personality. She was a young artist of far more than the average talent, and her charm of manner rendered her company sought after by a large circle of friends.

This lady complained to me that she suffered from the actual rudeness, nay, and almost positive brutality, of the crowds of persons thronging the busy streets of some of the principal thoroughfares of Paris. She complained that she was jostled here and there, and pushed rudely aside by the passing throng. Moreover, she was treated rudely in the shops, the superficial veneer of politeness of the average Parisian shop-clerk scarcely concealing the underlying contempt and veiled sneer of these "cheap" satellites of the ubiquitous shop-keepers of this charming city.

My first thought was that the young woman had worked herself up into a state of imaginary wrongs, the result of her highly sensitive organism and shrinking disposition — in short, I thought that she was suffering from a state of morbid self-consciousness, with its frequent accompaniment of imaginary persecution, etc. So I determined to test out the matter, and ascertain for myself just how much truth was in the case.

Making a slight change in my personal appearance, by means of a simple disguise once taught me by another of my students, a celebrated detective of Paris, I followed the young lady for several hours when she was on a shopping expedition. Much to my surprise, and, I may add, much to my indignation, I found that all that she had told me was correct. I could scarcely control myself at times, and more than once felt like chastising some rude fellow with my cane, so brutal was the conduct of certain individuals calling themselves "men."

There is a certain class of Parisian men, well dressed and with a veneer of polish, but boors and cures at heart. These men seem to take a special delight in jostling young women, almost pushing them off the sidewalks, at times, and in other ways earning a good caning at the hands of real gentlemen. Well, these cures seemed attracted to this sweet young girl, just as flies are drawn to a bit of sugar. They exceeded themselves in their display of rudeness and cowardly insolence, and all the while the girl was free from any outward appearance that would attract such cures naturally. I saw at once that there was some inner cause operating.

Moreover, I noticed that the young woman was also pushed aside rudely by hurrying businesspersons, who never glanced in her direction, but who thrust her aside as if she were an inanimate thing instead of a person. Again I found an inner cause. In the same way I found that she was treated exactly in the way she had complained of in the shops, by the clerks and shop-men, although she was a liberal customer, easily suited, and giving but little trouble. Here again, the inner trouble was apparent.

I went home and carefully diagnosed the case, and laid down a course or treatment. I sent for the young woman and told her that her trouble was a case of "ingrown sensitiveness, and overgrown modesty" — in short, that she had surrounded herself with an aura of self-depreciation and morbid sensitiveness. This aura practically invited persons to "pick on" her, to crowd her to the wall, to push her in the gutter, and to generally slight, snub and covertly insult her in the shops. Her aura was not only negative, but also actually attractively negative — that is to say, so negative that it actually attracted more positive natures in the direction of imposing on her weakness. (This is far from being unusual — it is a rule of the psychic as well as of the physical world, among animals as well as among men)

I immediately began teaching this lady the technique of the "direct flash" before the mirror (exactly as I have taught you), her flashes being invariably along the lines of positivism and strength. She would flash out "I am positive — far more positive than the crowd around me;" "Get out of my way, or I will walk over you;" "Clear the path for me, you vermin," and other exaggerated demands intended for the street crowds. In the same way she would flash out the command to the shop-people. "Come, now, I demand respectful attention;" "Lively, now, attend to my wants;" "I am a princess of the blood, bow to me, you underlings," etc. You will note that I purposely exaggerated the mental demands and flashes, because she needed an exaggerated positive mental attitude in order to overcome her natural and acquired handicap. In a short time she had acquired the technique perfectly and had developed a mental attitude and general personal atmosphere of a princess. Then she proceeded to "try it on the crowd," by means of the "positive aura."

The result was marvelous. From the moment her feet touched the sidewalks, her progress was that of a princess, persons instinctively moved out of her way, some even slightly bowing as they did so. The rowdy gentlemen (?) moved far away from her. And in the shops the queen of England could have received no more humble service or careful attention. The cure was complete, and has remained so. The young lady has long since laid aside the "Princess Royal" manner, and now simply maintains an aura of positive self-respect and self-confidence, and a demand that she be accorded the proper consideration.

Another case is that of a young student of mine — an American, the son of a prominent businessman. This young man was well educated, polished, and moreover, possessed of all the requisites of a successful salesman, except that of inspiring a feeling of friendship on the part of those with whom he came in contact. He was called upon to approach prominent businessmen in connection with his work for his father, and while he was able to present his arguments logically and forcibly, he was nevertheless handicapped by the fact the he repelled friendship, rather than invited it. In desperation, he made the trip across the Atlantic to consult me, and to beg a cure for his serious psychic trouble.

His cure was very easy. I simply put him through a course of the mirror exercises in the "direct flash," until he had mastered the technique; and then had him saturate his mind with the mental image and idea of: "You like me — you like me very much;" "You feel attracted toward me;" "You are my friend, and wish to show your friendship for me," etc., etc., etc. All these ideas were but variations of, an improvement upon, the simple idea of "You like me!"

Well, this young man began to radiate such an atmosphere of likability, friendship, etc., that he made friends right and left, even without tying — it was in the air around him, it seemed. His old trouble disappeared like magic — he was made over into a new man. And, yet it was all very simple, you see. Mere child's play, when one has the secret, as you now have. The young man insisted upon presenting me with his check for $1,000, although I had charged him but one-tenth of that amount, for my time and trouble.

I could go on in this vein, reciting case after case coming under my own experience, but I think that the two cases I have mentioned will give you the general idea of what I am trying to teach you, without my taking up more time and space at this point. The rule is general — it is for you to apply it to the particular requirements of your own case. Find out your weak spots of personal atmosphere, and then proceed to build up the opposite qualities of mind and character. Find out your negative points of attracting, and then proceed to build of their opposite positive qualities, just as the two students, just mentioned, did with such marked success. Read over carefully this chapter again, and again, until you get the point fixed in your mind. The rest is merely a matter of practice.

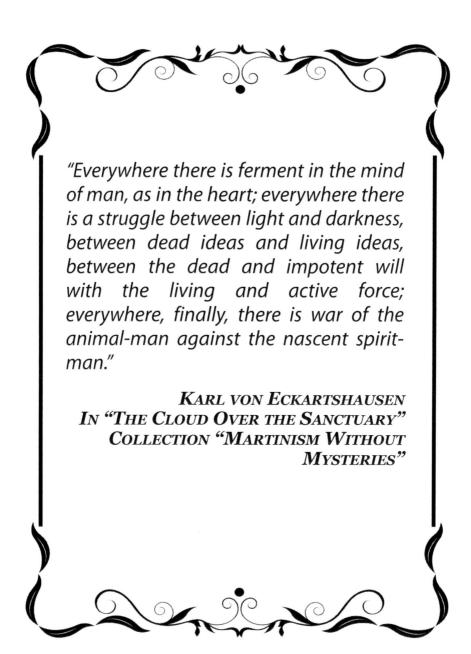

"Everywhere there is ferment in the mind of man, as in the heart; everywhere there is a struggle between light and darkness, between dead ideas and living ideas, between the dead and impotent will with the living and active force; everywhere, finally, there is war of the animal-man against the nascent spirit-man."

KARL VON ECKARTSHAUSEN IN "THE CLOUD OVER THE SANCTUARY" COLLECTION "MARTINISM WITHOUT MYSTERIES"

CHAPTER 17
THE DIRECT COMMAND

Having by this time acquired the technique of the "direct flash," by your mirror-practice; and having, also, mastered the art of cultivating the positive aura, you should be able to manifest what is known as "the direct command," without much additional instruction.

By "the direct command" is meant the flashing of a direct command or demand to the mind of another person, backed up by the concentrated power of both your mental and physical magnetism. Do you see now why I have first taught you to acquire the technique by means of the mirror-practice, and have then next taught you how to generate and maintain the positive aura? Certainly, you have seen the point! A moment's thought will show you that the "direct command" is really a combination of the methods of the mirror-practice, and that of the positive aura. The mirror-practice taught you the technique, and the practice afforded by the positive aura methods have served to give you ease, self-confidence, and an almost instinctive use of your magnetic powers in the direction of influencing other persons. You will also see the part played in your development by the special exercises in the direct flash, which I gave you in a preceding chapter. You now begin to see why I have led you to the present point by degrees, do you not?

The "direct command" is really a high form of the "direct flash," and is the method whereby the latter may be used to the highest degree of effectiveness.

In the "direct command" you flash your command to the mind of the other person, mentally, of course, but in exactly the same way that you would make an actual command by spoken words, if the conditions admitted of the same. You form the words of the command in your mind, carrying with it as strong a mental picture as you can create, and then mentally flash the command to the other person with as much magnetic force as you can muster.

∴

You will find it an aid to effectiveness, in the case of a contemplated demand upon some particular person, for a certain thing, to practice it before the mirror, using your own image as a "target" — just as you did in the exercise previously given you. You will find that a rehearsal of this kind will tend to increase your power at the time of the actual manifestation or command.

It is impossible to give you specific instruction for the carrying out of this program in special cases, for each person will have his or her own special requirements, the same depending upon the special circumstances of the case. All that I can do is to give you the general rules to your own particular cases and requirements. The general rules I have already given you.

Perhaps I can illustrate the application of the same by citing a few cases, which have actually come under my own observation and experience.

One of the most interesting cases of the kind that I have ever met with was that of a professor in one of the American universities. This man, a specialist in his particular line of scientific research, and a thorough master of his own particular subject, commanded a large audience of readers of his books and magazine articles, but, at the same time was almost a failure in his class work, owing to his inability to gain and hold the attention of his students. He came to me, in Paris, and explained his trouble. I gave him my short course in mental influence, etc., and drilled him well along the lines laid down in this book. I made him practice before an imaginary roomful of students, sending them a strong direct command of "Give me your full attention!" "Steady, now, your attention—your full and complete attention to my words!" and "That's right, you are giving me your full attention — now hold it firmly fixed on me!" and a similar stock of direct commands. These commands were directed commands were directed first to the "bellwethers" of the class — those natural leaders who are to be found in each class, and then scattered among the class at large. The professor told me that, after a number of these imaginary classroom scenes, each face being distinct and plain, and that he could almost see the flash of his command reaching them.

When I thought that he had mastered the general principles, and acquired the technique, I dismissed him, and he returned at once to the university in America. I received several letters from him during the following year, and he testified to the complete success of the plan when put into actual effect. From the first day of his return he obtained and held the attention of his class, and today he is one of the best personal instructors in his university, or elsewhere for that matter. In this case he applied the direct command to special individuals of the class, but the principle was the same as in the case of a single special individual, and differed from the positive aura method.

Another case was that of a promoter, now of international reputation, who formerly was unable to "close" many of his plans, owing to a lack of something in his mental makeup, he thought. He could evolve plans, which attracted the attention of prominent men and others, and he could also manage to fascinate them by his general talk regarding his enterprises. But he found it most difficult to induce them to take the final step to "coming in," or signing the contract, or entering the subscription, as the case might be.

I labored with this man, experiencing much trouble in overcoming his fixed and stubborn idea that there was, "something wrong" with his mental makeup. Finally, after a long period of careful drilling before an imaginary "prospect" (this term being applied to prospective customers) he began to feel that he had the missing element, after all. From that moment he was filled with new courage, and threw new life and energy into the exercises. So powerfully magnetic was this man, and so high a degree of concentrated force did he generate, that I could actually feel the force of his power while present in the room directing the exercises. I actually, myself, felt like subscribing to some of his stock, and am sure that had he approached me on the subject it would have required the exercise of my full power of self-protection and resistance to have overcome his magnetism.

When this man finished his instruction at my hands, he at once plunged into the floating of a new great enterprise, and carried the same to a most successful conclusion. He "closed" nearly every "prospect" that he approached, and soon dropped all the smaller "prospects," and devoted his entire attention to the "large fish." I do not feel at liberty to state here the exact words of the "direct command" used by him, for he paid me a large fee for my services, and the secret should be his own, under the circumstances—but this I will say, that his direct command was a straight out from the shoulder mental DEMAND upon the "prospect" to "come in."

Another interesting case was that of a now well-known actress, who lacked "fascination." She was a magnificent actress, of fine presence and a thorough knowledge of her art, but for some reason her acting seemed to lack soul. She came to me to learn how to influence her audience by personal magnetism, but I saw at once that her art, if fully exercised, would be sufficient to carry her audiences with her. Her trouble lay in the fact that there was a certain "fascination" lacking. I set her to work, training her so that she would actually fascinate the actors playing with her, and an air of reality would be thus created. She progressed rapidly, so quick were her perceptions. When she left me she was able to throw such a degree of fascination into her voice and manner, that the actor playing with her would be fairly swept off his feet; the result being that the audience would catch the same by a kind of mental contagion. She simply hurled mental direct commands at the actors, while reciting her lines, and while approaching them. Her success is now assured, but I cannot resist the temptation of mentioning that she has had the greatest trouble with her "leading men" in her companies—they all insist and persist in falling in love with her, and she has had to change them frequently to get rid of their unwelcome attentions, for her heart is "taken" elsewhere.

I fell that I am justified in calling the attention to another case — that of a leading statesman who took my instructions by means of a series of letters, several years ago. This man wanted MASTERY. He got it. I gave him the cue, and keynote, and he did the rest. So masterful did he become, by the employment of my suggested direct commands, that he dominated all who came near him. In fact he carried the thing a little too far—he grew to be regarded as dangerous and tyrannical, and powerful interests conspired against him. He is in temporary retirement at this time — but he is really but biding his time. It is impossible to remain in this man's presence for any time — particularly if his attention is directed toward you — without acknowledging him to be a MASTER.

I now ask you refer to the last pages of the chapter on the "direct flash." You will find there a number of sentences given as practices before the mirror. Study over these sentences carefully, and you will find therein a strong hint of the idea, which you should weave into your own direct commands. Students of mind, under my direction, have effectively employed all of these sentences; in actual practice—and all of them have the germ of success in them. You may use them singly, in combination, or as a general pattern around which you may weave your own ideas. Practice each of them, until you catch the spirit, and you will then have no trouble in creating your own commands in the most approved style. You will notice the DIRECTNESS and POSITIVENESS of each of these commands — these are the two essential qualities to be observed and used in this work of the direct command. Put all your magnetic force behind them, and flash them out right to the point—squarely into the mentality of the persons whom you wish to influence.

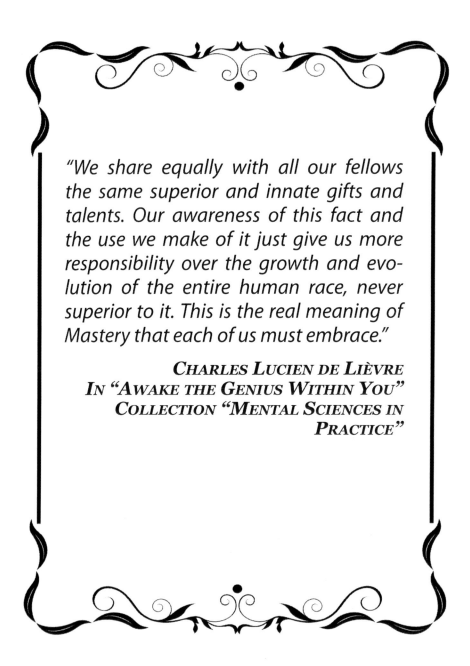

"We share equally with all our fellows the same superior and innate gifts and talents. Our awareness of this fact and the use we make of it just give us more responsibility over the growth and evolution of the entire human race, never superior to it. This is the real meaning of Mastery that each of us must embrace."

CHARLES LUCIEN DE LIÈVRE
IN "AWAKE THE GENIUS WITHIN YOU"
COLLECTION "MENTAL SCIENCES IN
PRACTICE"

CHAPTER 18

THE MAGNETIC DUEL

T he laws of personal magnetism are in accord with the other laws of nature in recognizing the universal fact that there are various degrees of power, and that, all else being equal, the stronger power will prevail over the weaker. But, it is likewise true that the individual, by a superior knowledge of the art of science of defense and offense, may often triumph over a superior degree of strength in the other person. This fact is as true of personal magnetism as it is of physical strength. The skilled magnetic individual may overcome his stronger adversary, just as the skilled boxer may overcome a stronger man, or a skilled fencer may disarm and defeat a much stronger opponent.

The conflict between the opposing magnetism of individuals is to be seen on all hands everyday. In fact, it has been well said that two persons never meet but that there is at least a preliminary trial of magnetic strength. At any rate, no two persons ever meet, whose interests are in the least opposed, but that there occurs a little tilt of magnetic strength — sometimes a quite strenuous test, in fact. And in these tests there always is one triumphant and one defeated. It is true that the circumstances of the case sometimes affect the result, and the defeated today may be the victor tomorrow, but the fact remains, that for the time being, at least, there is always one on top and the other underneath at the finish of the magnetic duel, be it slight or serious. One has but to recall incidents in their own experience to recognize this fact.

Oliver Wendell Holmes recognized this magnetic duel, in one of his books, when he speaks of "that deadly Indian hug in which men wrestle with their eyes, over in five seconds, but which breaks one of their two backs, and is good for three score years and ten, one trial enough — settles the whole matter — just as when two feathered songsters of the barnyard, game and dunghill, come together. After a jump or two, and a few sharp kicks, there is an end of it; and it is 'After you, monsieur' with the beaten party in all the social relations for all the rest of his days.

Dr. Fothergill, a well-known English Physician, now deceased, once wrote a little book upon the subject of the will. The good doctor was a close student of personal magnetism, although he did not choose to use the term itself in his writings, because of the narrow code of professional ethics then imposed upon the medical profession in Great Britain. I have personal magnetism, in theory and practice. I therefore take great pleasure in quoting from him on the particular subject now before us, as follows:

"The conflict of will, the power to command others, has been spoken of frequently. Yet what is this will power, which influences others? What is it that makes us accept, and adopt too, the advice of one person, while precisely the same advice from another has been rejected? Is it the weight or force of will, which insensibly influences us, the force of will behind the advice? That is what it is! The person who thus forces his or her advice upon us has no more power to enforce it than others; but all the same we do as requested. We accept from one what we reject from another. One person says of something contemplated, 'Oh, but you must not,' yet we do it all the same, though that person may be in a position to make us regret the rejection of that counsel. Another person says, 'Oh, but you mustn't,' and we desist, though we may, if so disposed, set this latter person's opinion defiance with impunity. It is not the fear of consequences, nor of giving offense, which determines the adoption of the latter person's advice, while it has been rejected when given by the first. It depends upon the character or willpower of the individual advising whether we accept the advice, or reject it. This character often depends little, if at all, in some cases, upon the intellect, or even on the moral qualities, the goodness or badness, of the individual. It is itself an imponderable something; yet it carries weight with it.

There may be abler men, cleverer men; but it is the one possessed of will who rises to the surface at these times — the one who can by some subtle power make other men obey him.

The will-struggle goes on universally. In the young aristocrat, who gets his tailor to make another advance in defiance of his conviction that he will never get his money back? It goes on between lawyer and client; betwixt doctor and patient; between banker and borrower; betwixt buyer and seller. It is not tact, which enables the person behind the counter to induce customers to buy what they did not intend to buy, and which when bought, gives them no satisfaction, though it is linked therewith for the effort to be successful.

Whenever two persons meet in business, or in any other relation in life, up to lovemaking, there is this will-fight going on, commonly enough without any consciousness of the struggle. There is a dim consciousness of the result, but none of the processes. It often takes years of the intimacy of married life to find out with whom of the pair the mastery really lays. Often the far stronger character, to all appearances, has to yield; it is this will-element, which underlies the statement. 'The race is not always to the swift, nor the battle to the strong.' In 'Middlemarch' we find in Lydgate a grand aggregation of qualities, yet shallow, hard, selfish Rosamond masters him thoroughly in the end. He was not deficient in will power, possessed more than an average share of character; but in the fight he went down at last under the onslaught of the intense, stubborn will of his narrow-minded spouse. Their will-contest was the collision of a large, warm nature, like a capable human hand, with a hard, narrow, selfish nature, like a steel button; the hand only bruised itself while the button remained unaffected."

If you will substitute the term "magnetic force," for "will," "will power," etc., in the good doctor's words, you will see how perfectly he was in accord with the teachings contained in this book.

The student who has carefully studied the foregoing pages will have acquired sufficient knowledge of the theory and practice, the method and the technique of personal magnetism to be able to carry himself or herself though a "magnetic duel" with credit to himself or herself, and credit to myself, the teacher. But remember, that there is as much in adroitness, and skill, as there is in mere strength of magnetism. Carry in mind the tactics of the good boxer, or good fencer — try to reproduce (in the magnetic duel) the guards, the feints, the unexpected stroke, the rushes, the overpowering stroke, etc. It will not hurt you to purposely engage in some of these conflicts, as good practice preparing for the day of a real test of power on some important point. Assert your will a little, and strive to have your own way in small matters, particularly if you are opposed therein by others. The skill and practice, together with the self-confidence you will gain will prove useful to you in the hour or need.

In addition to the general and special instruction regarding the use of positive magnetism in relation to other persons, I now offer for your consideration the following special "flashes," for use on special occasions, especially in cases of the "magnetic duel." You will find these flashes of great use to you on such occasions, particularly (as is generally the case) where the opponent does not know the secret of his own natural power of magnetism, and is not versed in the art and science of using it. Study over these carefully — for they are valuable, and represent the result of years of experience and practice. Here follows the list just spoken of: "My magnetism is stronger than yours — it is overpowering you."

"My magnetism is beating down your guard — you are weakening."

"I am more positive than you — you are negative and are beginning to retreat and give in to me."

"You are beginning to feel afraid of me, afraid, afraid, afraid of me."

"Retreat, retreat, retreat, I tell you — I am forcing you backward."

"I am scattering your forces — I am dissipating your energy — I am breaking your magnetism to bits, by the power of my own force."

"I am standing on the solid rock of power — your feet are on sand, and are slipping way from you."

"GET OUT OF MY WAY — I COMMAND YOU TO GET OUT!"

"I am crowding you back, off your feet; move back, I tell you — BACK, out of my way, I tell you!"

You may get the spirit of the above by carefully reading them, repeating them to your image in the mirror, throwing full fore into the words, and the expression into your eyes. Then you will be able to flash them out to others when the occasion arises, with ease, power and effect. You need not be bound by the precise words that I have given you, providing you catch the spirit behind them. You may use your own words — the very words that you would like to actually utter to the other person, if you prefer. The thing to do is to get the feeling and meaning into his mind.

In a succeeding chapter, entitled "Magnetic Self-Defense," you will find full instruction for defensive flashes, and "guards," which are to be used in connection with the above offensive ones, in the magnetic duel. Beat the opponent off by neutralizing his magnetism, according to the advice given in the next chapter, and then plunge in your own mental weapons of attack. The following constitutes a broad-sword mental weapon, which may often be used with the greatest effect:

"I am pouring into you a strong concentrated current of magnetic power. Which is overpowering you and conquering you, and bending you to my will. My magnetism is far stronger than is yours, and I know how to use it to better advantage than do you. I am overpowering you — I am conquering you — I am bending you to my will. I am MASTERING you, steadily and completely. I shall command you to do as I will. You MUST do it, and do it now. Surrender, I tell you — surrender now — SURRENDER to me at once. You MUST, and you SHALL. I am breaking down your resistance. You are giving up — SURRENDER NOW — SURRENDER AT ONCE."

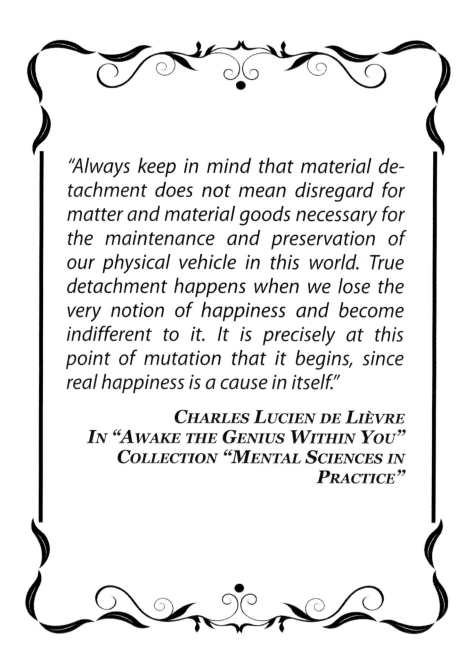

"Always keep in mind that material detachment does not mean disregard for matter and material goods necessary for the maintenance and preservation of our physical vehicle in this world. True detachment happens when we lose the very notion of happiness and become indifferent to it. It is precisely at this point of mutation that it begins, since real happiness is a cause in itself."

CHARLES LUCIEN DE LIÈVRE
IN "AWAKE THE GENIUS WITHIN YOU"
COLLECTION "MENTAL SCIENCES IN
PRACTICE"

CHAPTER 19

CORPOREAL MAGNETISM

Before concluding my instruction regarding the subject of the projection of personal magnetism, I wish to have a few words with you on the subject of what may be called "corporeal" magnetism. By "corporeal' is meant, "pertaining to the body." I use the term "corporeal magnetism" to indicate and designate the conveyance of personal magnetism by means of physical contact, as, for instance, by the touch of the hands, lips, etc.

It may be objected to that this term is needless, inasmuch as I have already considered the phase of physical magnetism, or nerve-force, in connection with the general subject of personal magnetism. But, I answer; by "corporeal magnetism" I mean something different from mere physical magnetism, or nerve-force. The new term is far more inclusive, for, by "corporeal magnetism" I mean the projection of the combined personal magnetism (physical and mental) to the other person, over the channels of the nervous system of both persons, instead of through the ether as in the case of the ordinary projection of personal magnetism.

Note this distinction: Under the head of physical magnetism, I explained to you how magnetic healing treatments might be given by the use of the hands, the physical magnetism passing over the nervous system of the healer, making the leap between the finger-tips and the body of the other person. But, in "corporeal magnetism" not only the physical magnetism or nerve-force, is so projected to the other person, but at the same time is also projected the mental magnetism. In short, the entire process of the projection of combined personal magnetism is performed, but the magnetism flows along physical channels, instead of across the ether, to reach the other person. I trust that you clearly perceive this distinction, before we proceed further.

That there exists this phase of personal magnetism, called "corporal magnetism" cannot be doubted by the careful investigator. On all sides we may see evidence of the phenomena of this phase of personal magnetism. In the handshake of the person is often conveyed the strongest kind of personal magnetism — in the touch of the hand is often found the strongest kind of emotional vibrations. In the kiss, and the contact of the cheek, are often to be found the most active form of emotional vibrations, as almost everyone knows. In short, by bodily contact there may often be conveyed the most dangerous forms of sexual magnetism — and other forms of magnetism.

I do not intend to say much regarding sexual magnetism in this book, but I would not be doing justice to my students if I failed to at least mention some plain facts, in passing. I need scarcely remind my student of the powerful sexual emotions often aroused by a kiss, or touch of the cheek, or even the "holding of hands" — this knowledge is common to the race, although few understand the real nature of the phenomena. Enough for me to say that the libertine generally realizes full well the powerful vibrations, which may be conveyed in this manner, although he does not understand the scientific facts of the case — he has the practice well defined in his mind, although he does not understand the theory. Young persons, especially young women, should be taught the danger of this form of magnetism, and should avoid allowing the physical contact which makes the same active. The "holding hands," the thoughtless kiss, pressure of the cheek, embrace, or close physical contact, all afford and furnish a "direct line" for the passage of this form of magnetism, i.e., the sexual magnetism conveyed through corporeal channels. The unprincipled person, of strong passions, soon learns that by close physical contact he may often convey his emotional vibration to the young woman, and thus arouse reciprocal vibrations, which may sweep her off her feet, and into his arms — often to her utter ruin and disgrace. This is not a pleasant subject, but I feel that I would not be true to my students if I failed to point out this dangerous force, and to caution them to guard against the employment of the same against them.

Leaving this phase of the subject, I now wish to call the attention of my students to the use of corporeal magnetism in the ordinary use of the hands, as in shaking hands, etc. Here is a subject worthy of the closest attention on your part.

Strongly magnetic men, and those who have studied this subject, frequently employ this method of projecting personal magnetism in making their preliminary moves in the direction of influencing other persons by personal magnetism. Who has not experienced the magnetic handshake of individuals of this kind? And, on the other hand, who has not been conscious of the feeling of repulsion inspired by the cold, clammy, snake-like handshake of other types of persons?

You have also probably noticed that many men whose business it is to influence you in any direction, such as politicians, preachers, promoters, salesmen, etc., have a habit of placing their hands upon your shoulders, during the conversation — or laying their hand lightly on your arm while speaking to you — in some cases, giving you a final pat on the back as they urge you to "sign right here, and close the thing up." Have you realized that this is a form of corporal magnetism, and that the result is often very effective? Look out for these fellows in the future, and neutralize their magnetism according to the rules given in the next chapter of this book. If you choose to employ these methods yourself — well, that is your own business, and a matter for yourself to decide. It is a very strong method of conveying corporeal magnetism, I assure you.

In shaking hands with any person whom you may wish to influence, you should throw into the clasp the strongest possible kind of personal magnetism, physical and mental, according to the rules already given you in this book. Give the person the direct command at the moment of the clasp, throwing it into him by means of the nerves of the hand and fingers. (A little practice, in the direction of shaking hands with yourself will be of great aid to you in this matter). Send him a mental message just as you would if you were merely looking at him.

When you meet a person with whom you are acquainted, the handclasp is the natural thing, and it gives you a splendid opportunity to get in a powerful preliminary flash of personal magnetism, accompanied by the strongest possible direct command. When this is performed properly, it will serve to get the other person in exactly the right psychic conditions to receive your further direct commands, and to yield more readily to your magnetism. It is your "advance guard" preparing the way for the grand charge upon the breast-works of the enemy. Use it well and half the battle will be won at one stroke.

Always be hearty in your handclasp — not rough or too strenuous, for no one likes to have his hand tightly squeezed or bruised — always remember the word "hearty" in this connection. Beware of the lifeless handshake — throw feeling into it, and make it be alive and vital. Shake hands as if the other person meant something to you, and hold on to his hand for a moment, and then let go as if with reluctance. Seek out some strongly magnetic person, used to meeting people — some successful politician, for instance — and let him shake hands with you. Notice how much interest and feeling he puts into his clasp — and then take notes from his methods. A good magnetic preacher, meeting his flock at the church door as they pass out, also will give you a good example. Study them and "catch the motion."

When shaking hands with a person who you wish to influence, you should throw into the handclasp the direct command, which you wish to impress upon him. If you wish him, or her, to like you, your direct command should be along those lines, for instance, a strong "You LIKE me!" If you wish to assert your positivity over his power, you should get to work at once with a very strong positive "I am stronger than you," or "I am far more POSITIVE than you!" or some other statement of the same general kind, such as I have given you in the preceding chapters. In fact, you may use nay or all of the statements previously given to you, in this form as well as in the ordinary phases of the direct command.

In concluding this chapter, I wish to call your attention to a phase of the phenomena of corporeal magnetism, which is often overlooked by teachers of the subject. I allude to that form of magnetism, which is projected by mere "nearness" of the bodies of persons, even though direct contact may not be had. Good salesmen and others often know this from their own experience, although not understanding the real cause. They know that by sitting near to the customer, they can get a better magnetic effect than if compelled to sit at a little distance. The result of the "heart to heart" talk often results from this nearness. In the same way, the gestures of the hands of a speaker, coming in close contact to other persons, often serves to convey the magnetism to them, although no actual contact is had.

The hands, particularly, are very effective instruments for the conveyor of corporeal magnetism, for the nerves of the fingers are very sensitive, and readily convey and project the magnetism with great concentrated force. The use of the fingers of the mesmerist is but one example of this fact. You will also notice that the majority of effective orators and speakers have a way of making passes and waves at their audiences. The good solicitor or promoter usually employs his hands in this way. Remember, I do not say that these people are always conscious of the facts behind their gestures — they often are ignorant of the same, and use their hands instinctively, having acquired the movements through habit. But the facts remain, and those who learn the secret of the force and its employ-ment, and thereafter use it consciously and delibera-tely, are placed at a great advantage over others who do not possess this knowledge. And, mark my words, there are thousands of the worlds greatest men who have learned this secret, taken lessons in its use, and are now employing it actively. You may now join their ranks, if you care to do so.

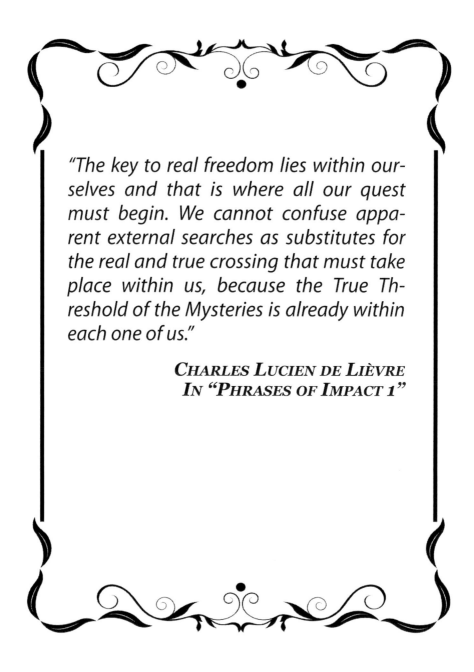

"The key to real freedom lies within ourselves and that is where all our quest must begin. We cannot confuse apparent external searches as substitutes for the real and true crossing that must take place within us, because the True Threshold of the Mysteries is already within each one of us."

CHARLES LUCIEN DE LIÈVRE
IN "PHRASES OF IMPACT 1"

CHAPTER 20

MAGNETIC SELF-DEFENSE

And, now, having acquainted you with the various forms of the manifestation, projection and use of personal magnetism — having taught you not only the theory, but also the practice; not only how to acquire the technique, but also how to effectively employ the same — I will conclude by calling your attention to the defensive side of the question. In boxing or fencing, you have not mastered the art fully until you are able not only to attack, but also, how to defend — not only the art of aggressive action, but also the science of defensive action. And, so it is in the case of personal magnetism, you must not only know how to use the force in the form of projection, but you must also know how to defend yourself against the projection of the force by others.

It is true that the careful and diligent student of these lessons will gradually develop such a power within himself that he will scarcely ever meet individuals more powerful than himself. But, still, there are always the very strong individuals to be reckoned with, and I want you to possess the secret of dispersing and dissipating the magnetism of such persons, so far as effect on yourself is concerned, by the methods known to all advanced students and practitioners of personal magnetism.

This defensive science is far simpler than you would think at first, although to be effective in the same you must first have learned how to project effectively. I may sum it up in a few words — heed them carefully. The secret is this: In defending one-self against magnetic projection in any or all of its forms, you have but to project toward the other person a strong DENIAL of his power to influence, affect, or master you. That is the whole thing in a nutshell. Now for the details.

But, right here, I want to remind you of a very important fact, and that is in this denial you do not really destroy or lessen the power of the other person, in general. You only neutralize his magnetism so far as it affects yourself, or those whom you wish to protect. In other words, instead of destroying his weapons, you merely turn them aside, and cause them to glance off, leaving you, and yours, harmless. To use a familiar illustration from the field of electricity, you render yourself a non-conductor, and the force glances off you without affecting you in the slightest. Remember this illustration, and you will have the idea firmly fixed in your mind.

You may render yourself immune not only from the direct flash, and direct demand or command, of others, no matter how strong they may be; but also from the general contagion of the mental atmosphere or auras of others. By proper concentrated effort, along these lines, you may render yourself absolutely immune from the force of the personal magnetism of others, if you so desire. Or, if you prefer, you may shut out only certain individuals from your field, and allow the beneficial magnetism of others to enter it. In truth, you are your own MASTER, if you but exert your power.

As to the methods to be employed, you have but to use those you have already learned in these lessons, by merely changing the mental attitude and statement or command. For instance, instead of projecting the direct command that you are stronger than the other person, and can therefore influence him; you have but to calmly DENY his power over you, and defy him to affect you in the slightest. As a matter of fact, that mental attitude is far less strenuous than the aggressive form of magnetic projection. It requires merely the interposition of your magnetic shield of defense, and his power will glance off without affecting you, even though he is most strenuously projecting it. There is of course the other plan of fighting aggressive magnetism with aggressive magnetism — this is the real magnetic duel in its plain form, and may be used when desired. But if you merely wish to repel the aggression of others, you have but to use the defensive plan of the DENIAL, as I have just told you.

In forming the mental statement, which accompanies all forms of the use of mental magnetism, as you have seen, you merely express (mentally) in a few, strong positive words, the idea you wish to reach the other person's mind. Well, so it is the case of magnetic self-defense. You simply mentally state in a few strong words that you deny the power of the other person. You will find, as you experiment, that in the very words "I DENY," there is a mighty dynamic power of defense. It is the mental idea behind these words, which, figuratively wipes out of existence the other person's magnetism, at least so far as you are concerned. It is the great SHIELD OF DEFENSE. Let the full meaning of the word "DENY" enter into your mind — you will find it contains a new meaning and strength, when considered in this connection.

Now, right at this point, before proceeding further, I ask you to turn back over the leaves of the preceding lessons, and make note of the numerous statements given to accompany the positive aura, the direct flash, the direct command, etc. Then from within your own mind, the denial of these statements (if they are projected by another person), and you will find that you possess instinctively the power to frame such statements of denial, easily. Practice a little, imagining that another person is hurling these flashes or commands at you, and that you are interposing the shield of denial in each case. You will be surprised, and delighted, to realize how easily you can repel the strongest of these assaults. You may then begin to practice by throwing yourself into the presence and company of the strongest magnetic persons you know, and then see how easily you can repel their power — and how free, calm and serene you now feel in their presence.

There are two things to be remembered in this connection — I have already told you them, but it is well to repeat them in order to fix them firmly in your mind. I ask you to consider them in the following paragraphs.

In the first place, as I have told you, this defensive process merely enables you to throw off and render yourself immune from the aggressive magnetism of others — it does not enable you to master them or to compel them to do your bidding. In order to accomplish the latter, you must beat down the guard of the other person; protect yourself at the same time; and then carry the day by a direct magnetic assault upon him. You can do these things if he fights you with the weapons of aggressive magnetism only, but if he DENY your power, he is immune, and you cannot affect him; just as if you DENY his power, you are immune — in case both DENY, then the battle is drawn, and neither win. The Denial is not a weapon of aggressiveness — it is merely the shield of defense. Remember this! Of course, if you use both shield and sword, you will have a double advantage, providing he does not also use the shield. For if you can repel his magnetism, and at the same time use your own — then he is at your mercy. But if he knows enough to also use his shield — then the battle will be drawn, and neither will win a decided victory. Do you catch the idea? Think over it until it is plain to you.

The second point I wish to impress upon you, in this connection, is the fact, already stated by me, that you do not actually destroy or weaken the other person's magnetism, by the use of the shield of denial. His magnetism remains just as strong, and just as much in evidence, as if you did not use the shield — the only difference being that by using it you render his weapons powerless against you, or those you may wish to protect; and thus create immunity for yourself, and your protégés, by interposing the shield of defense. But you do not impair the power of the other person against others whom you do not directly shelter behind your shield. Do you get this point? Think over it until you get it clearly.

When you repel the magnetism of one of the persons who have been using it without knowing the nature of his power (and there are many who so use it — the majority of persons, in fact) you will be amused to see how "broken up" such a person becomes. He will become bewildered at his failure to influence and affect you, and will often become embarrassed and, in some cases, actually entangled in the currents of his own magnetism. It may even happen (it often does, really) that such a person will become so confused by his apparent loss of power, that he will lose his assurance and consequently his ability to attack. In such cases, he becomes an easy subject for a magnetic rush or broadside on your own part, which will quickly drive him into a disastrous retreat. Of course, if he has a scientific knowledge of the subject, he will not be so taken off guard, but, recognizing your knowledge and power, he will pass it off with a smile, and relinquish the attack.

And, now, good student, we part company for the present. I am glad to have had the honor of giving you this instruction, in these lessons, and I trust that you will so conduct yourself that you will be a creditable pupil of mine, and do me honor by your accomplishments and attainments. I have supplied you with the weapons of both aggressive and also of defensive personal magnetism, and have taught you how to employ both of them so as to get the best results. It is now "up to you" to make the best use of these weapons, according to the rule and principles which I have laid down for your guidance.

In parting, I wish to again impress two important rules upon you, and these are:

(1) Practice, practice, practice, until you have every detail of the instruction so well learned, and so fixed by habit, that you can and will use them instinctively, just as you now walk, or breathe, or speak.

(2) Keep your own secrets, and do not dissipate and scatter your influence by hinting of your secrets of

your power over others. There are many good reasons for this rule — some reasons that do not appear on the surface, by the way. Remember the old Italian proverb: "In bocca chiusa, non c'entra mosca" – that is to say: "Into the closed mouth, no flies enter." Heed the spirit of the proverb.

Au revoir, my magnetic friends — we shall meet again, in due time.

*Theron **Q.** Dumont*

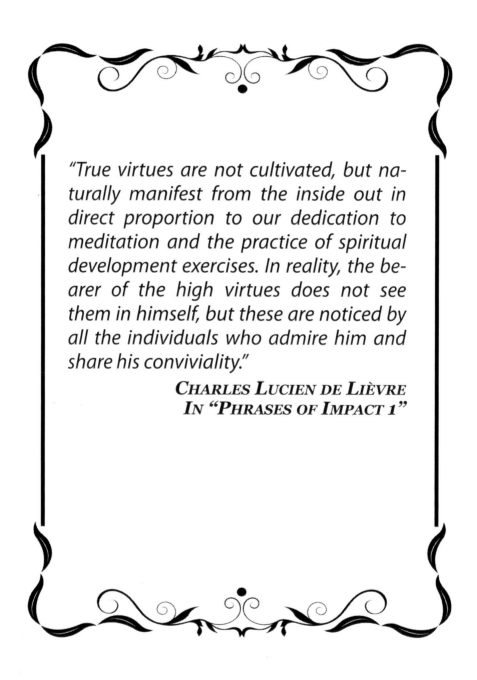

"True virtues are not cultivated, but naturally manifest from the inside out in direct proportion to our dedication to meditation and the practice of spiritual development exercises. In reality, the bearer of the high virtues does not see them in himself, but these are noticed by all the individuals who admire him and share his conviviality."

CHARLES LUCIEN DE LIÈVRE
IN "PHRASES OF IMPACT 1"

Made in United States
North Haven, CT
04 November 2022

26286469R00122